PEN

V.

John Gillingham is Emeritus Professor of Medieval History at the London School of Economics. His books include a biography of Richard I, *The Angevin Empire* and *The English in the Twelfth Century*.

JOHN GILLINGHAM

William II

The Red King

PENGUIN BOOKS

PENGUIN BOOKS

UK | USA | Canada | Ireland | Australia
India | New Zealand | South Africa

Penguin Books is part of the Penguin Random House group of companies
whose addresses can be found at global.penguinrandomhouse.com.

First published by Allen Lane 2015
First published in Penguin Books 2019

001

Set in 9.5/13.5 pt Sabon LT Std
Typeset by Jouve (UK), Milton Keynes
Printed and bound in Great Britain by Clays Ltd, Elcograf S.p.A.

ISBN: 978–0–141–98988–4

www.greenpenguin.co.uk

Contents

WILLIAM II

For Kate, Emma and Brenda

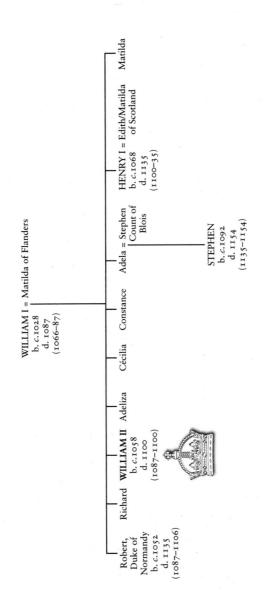

WILLIAM I = Matilda of Flanders
b. c.1028
d. 1087
(1066–87)

Robert, Duke of Normandy
b. c.1052
d. 1135
(1087–1106)

Richard

WILLIAM II
b. c.1058
d. 1100
(1087–1100)

Adeliza

Cécilia

Constance

Adela = Stephen Count of Blois

HENRY I = Edith/Matilda of Scotland
b. c.1068
d. 1135
(1100–35)

Matilda

STEPHEN
b. c.1092
d. 1154
(1135–1154)

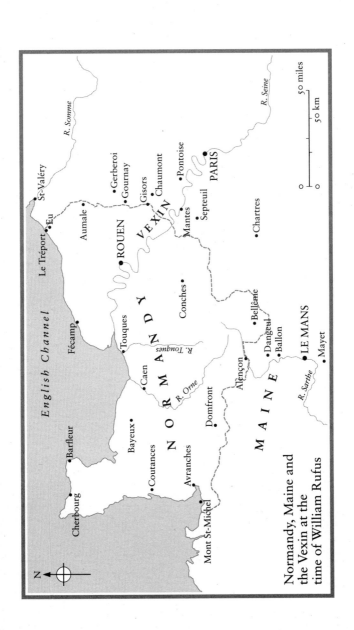

Normandy, Maine and the Vexin at the time of William Rufus

William II

I
The Personality of the King:

EVIDENCE AND INTERPRETATIONS

'This monarch was always very angry and red in the face
and was therefore unpopular, so that his death was a Good
Thing: it occurred in the following memorable way. Rufus
was hunting one day in the New Forest . . .' These words,
the opening of the chapter on William II in Sellar and Yeat-
man's 1066 *and All That*, still represent the sum of what is
widely known about the king who ruled England from
1087 to 1100: that he died in the New Forest in controversial circumstances. Son of and successor to William the
Conqueror, the Norman duke whose conquest of England
in 1066 made him a key figure in the shaping of English
history, the Red King inevitably stands in his father's
shadow, referred to by his contemporaries as William jun-
ior. Moreover the later years of his reign coincided with the
First Crusade and the capture of Jerusalem (1096–9). By
comparison with that extraordinary series of events in the
minds of those who lived through them, William II's
exploits paled into insignificance. In consequence, as far
as most people are concerned, only the mystery of Rufus's
death – was it a hunting accident, assassination or ritual
killing? – brings him suddenly and briefly into a narrow
shaft of light.

Here I am much more interested in his life and reign than in his death. Just a boy when his father conquered England, he lived through a turbulent period, coming to the throne while the overwhelming consequences of the Norman Conquest were still unravelling. Few kings of England have faced a more testing legacy: as the Norman son of a Norman father he headed a regime that spoke a language which the great majority of his subjects did not understand. An English monk, Eadmer of Canterbury, bitterly contrasted the career prospects of natives and newcomers: 'If they were English,' he wrote, 'no virtue was enough to secure their promotion; if they were foreigners, the mere appearance of virtue was enough for them to be awarded the highest honour.'[1] Only one year before William II's accession, a projected Danish invasion had been intended to free the English from Norman rule. In 1098 the Earl of Shrewsbury was killed on Anglesey while fighting King Magnus of Norway. There was no telling when the next Scandinavian king would return to take up King Cnut's inheritance. No one had been told that the Viking Age was over.

The occupying regime was itself deeply divided. William II's claim to the throne was disputed by his older brother, Robert, and a majority of the most powerful landowners in England were prepared to go to war on Robert's behalf. In the event William triumphantly overcame these and other challenges. 'He had such success in defeating his enemies and in acquiring territories that you would suppose the whole world smiled upon him,' wrote Eadmer. 'Even the wind and the sea appeared to obey him.'[2] But he had his critics, chiefly among churchmen, and when he was unexpectedly killed at the height of his power, they saw in this a death sentence passed upon him by God. In their eyes God's judgment proved that, for all his successes, William II was fundamentally an evil man and a bad ruler.

By far the most influential statement of this view came in two books written by Eadmer: *The History of Novelties in England* (*Historia Novorum in Anglia*) and *The Life of Anselm Archbishop of Canterbury* (*Vita Anselmi Archiepiscopi*). Completed after Anselm's death in 1109, both presented the archbishop as a champion of reform and of the freedom of the Church in principled opposition to a tyrannical king. Such was Anselm's saintliness that, according to Eadmer, the stone coffin in which he was laid, at first too small, grew in size until it could accommodate his whole body. But the evidence of the letters which Anselm wrote in the 1090s suggests that the relationship between king and archbishop was nowhere near the dramatic clash of principles presented by Eadmer. Nonetheless the leading historians of the next generation, William of Malmesbury, Orderic Vitalis and Henry of Huntingdon, all three writing in Latin, all ecclesiastics, two of them monks, were deeply influenced by Eadmer's presentation of the reign as a struggle between a wicked king and a holy archbishop. Other twelfth-century authors, notably Geoffrey Gaimar and Wace – men writing in French, the language which Rufus and his friends spoke – saw things very differently. In Gaimar's eyes Rufus was a model king, a fine warrior, a lion feared by his neighbours and a good-humoured and generous monarch who did much for the internal well-being of his kingdom, ruling strongly and keeping the peace. 'Never',

Gaimar wrote, 'was there a king held in such affection or in such honour by his men.'[3]

Yet the views of those who admired Rufus came to be disregarded, while the opinions of his critics stuck. It is not that men and women such as Gaimar and his patron, Lady Constance fitzGilbert were uninfluential figures in their own day. Elite secular culture was both dominant and self-confident. Eadmer remarked that long-haired and courtly aristocrats mocked those who cut their hair short, calling them peasants or priests, both evidently terms of abuse. But as far as subsequent generations of learned scholars were concerned, Gaimar and Wace wrote in the 'frivolous' medium of French verse, and their work came to be either forgotten or dismissed as not 'serious history'. Gaimar's *Estoire* lay unseen for more than six hundred years until it was disinterred in the nineteenth century, and it was then ignored for another 150 years – not surprisingly since it was so 'obviously wrong' in its assessment of Rufus. Only recently have historians begun to re-evaluate Gaimar's testimony. For almost nine hundred years it was the monks' view of Rufus which came to be the accepted truth about this king.

Rufus was particularly unlucky in that the most detailed and apparently authoritative account of his reign was composed by an author who was arguing a case. Eadmer's purpose in writing *The History of Novelties* was, he stated, to describe 'the grievous calamity which overtook the churches of England'.[4] Moreover, as William of Malmesbury, himself a master of Latin style, wrote, Eadmer possessed the rare gift of 'expounding things so lucidly that it all seems to be happening before our very eyes'.[5] Not only before our eyes. In Eadmer's rendering of arguments between archbishop and king, we can hear their voices. In one case no less than twelve quick-fire exchanges between them end with Rufus saying: 'Your predecessor would never have dared say such things to my father. I shall do nothing for you.'[6]

Of these two images, the ecclesiastical and the secular, which one came closer to the 'real Rufus'? Even supposing that such a person as the 'real Rufus' had ever existed, there is, of course, no way of knowing for sure. At all times powerful people are likely to provoke opposing opinions, sometimes violently so. But three approaches offer the possibility of getting a little closer to the character of the king. The first is to give greater weight to words written before his death than after it. Unfortunately almost everything we think we know about his life comes from words written after 1100. Of all the reigns since the Norman Conquest, William II's is the least well recorded. There are long periods, such as the two years from Christmas 1088 until Christmas 1090, when we have no idea where Rufus was. We know of only one chronicler active in England during his lifetime, an anonymous continuator of the king-centred set of annals written in English known as the *Anglo-Saxon Chronicle*. He was well informed, and wanted us to know that he was. In his obituary of Rufus's father he proclaimed that he was writing of him 'even as we, who have looked upon him, and once lived at his court, have perceived him'.[7] Although it is highly probable that most of the annals for Rufus's reign were composed not long after the end of the year in question, several reflect a degree of hindsight, such as the observation, under the year 1091, that an agreement between the king and his brother Robert 'lasted only a little while'. His obituary of Rufus, culminating in the assertion that he 'was hated by almost all his people and abhorrent to God, exactly as his end proved, because he died his injustice unabated and without him repenting or making any amends', bears witness to the impact the king's unexpected death had on the assessment of his character.

Another work written during the 1090s is an account of the miracles attributed to Saint Edmund. Its author, Herman of Bury St Edmunds, tells us that the king, whom he mentions only in passing, was known as 'Longsword'. It is symptomatic of the way in which views of the king set down during his lifetime have been blanked out by later ones that 'Longsword' has been all but forgotten. Instead the king is remembered by the nickname first known to have been used at least fifteen years after his death by two authors writing in northern France: Orderic Vitalis and Guibert de Nogent. In Gaimar he was the 'rus rei', the red king. According to Wace, the name Rufus was invented in order to distinguish him from his father. That practice has made sense to all subsequent historians and will be followed here.

Two short tracts written early in his reign and presumably intended to have an immediate political impact have survived, despite their ephemeral character. One is a brief account of Rufus's succession, probably composed on the new king's behalf. The second is a much more valuable document: a narrative of the trial of the Bishop of Durham in November 1088 on a charge of treason, arguably the most vivid account of a state trial in eleventh-century Europe. Written by someone on the bishop's side, it nonetheless portrays Rufus acting as a king was expected to, taking counsel with advisers chosen from the most powerful in the realm, ecclesiastics as well as laymen. For the most part Rufus's case against the bishop is presented by spokesmen, but occasionally the king himself intervenes forcefully, his words reported in direct speech. This strictly contemporary narrative confirms what later writers tell us: that Rufus liked to speak briefly and sharply. Many medieval chroniclers put words into the mouths of kings. But almost always they give them eloquent speeches, which might reflect the content of the king's opinions but in style are clearly the authors' own rhetorical products. By contrast the words they put into Rufus's mouth look as though they genuinely reflected his way of speaking.

The political culture of the time was fundamentally an oral one. Kings transmitted their decisions and commands by word of mouth much more often than in writing. Those which were written down survived only if, and for as long as, the recipients kept them. Not until the late twelfth century did the English government begin to archive copies of outgoing documents. Hence very few royal records survive from Rufus's reign, in total not much more than two hundred documents, compared with about six times as many for his brother Henry I's much longer reign (1100–35). In any case documents such as charters are formulaic and inevitably conceal whatever individuality the king possessed. A few contemporary political letters survive, including two which were written in reply to ones sent in the king's name.

One of these, composed by the most famous canon lawyer of the day, Ivo of Chartres, offers a tantalizing glimpse of Rufus's own thoughts, but of his letters themselves not one remains. Most of the surviving letters in which he is mentioned were written by Anselm, and kept as part of the developing cult of 'saint' Anselm. Some of these reveal that relations between king and archbishop were not always as bad as Eadmer made out later.

A second approach is to deal with post-1100 evidence by highlighting those attributes which were emphasized by both admirers and critics. One was Rufus's capacity to command success in war. Another was his sense of humour. For Eadmer, this consisted of mocking and sarcastic jokes that revealed his lack of respect for serious men and subjects; for Gaimar, Rufus's ready laughter defused tensions among his leading subjects.

A third approach is to make an effort to see through and beyond the explicit messages which chroniclers presented, both for and against Rufus, in order to focus on what they unintentionally reveal. Take Orderic Vitalis, for example, the greatest chronicler of Norman life in the Middle Ages. As a monk, a member of the community of Saint-Evroul since 1085, Orderic shared the opinion of those who declared that William II's sudden death in 1100 was God's punishment for his oppression of the Church and his refusal to listen to those priests who urged him to renounce a vicious and squalid way of life. 'He never married, but was insatiably addicted to obscene fornication and frequent adulteries, giving his subjects a damnable example of shameful debauchery.'[8]

Yet Orderic retained so clear a memory of a widely popular king with an attractively easygoing manner that he could not resist describing what happened at the Norman port of Touques one July day in 1099 as people gathered, as they often did in summer, to watch ships come in and hear the latest news. On this occasion they were astonished to learn that the king himself was on board the ship just in from England. Normal practice was for the arrival of important people to be heralded well in advance, so that proper preparations could be made; but this time Rufus, having crossed the Channel in haste in order to deal with a crisis which had blown up at Le Mans, arrived unannounced. On landing he acted as his own herald, laughing cheerfully as he answered the crowd's questions. Amid general joy he then mounted a horse belonging to a local priest and rode on to Bonneville-sur-Touques, escorted by a throng of clergy and country people running alongside and applauding.[9]

New and better editions of the chroniclers' narratives have allowed the preoccupations and rhetorical techniques of twelfth-century opinion-makers to be analysed more closely. In writing, for instance, of 'the monks' view' of Rufus, I have oversimplified. Not all monks were quite that simple. One who most certainly was not was William of Malmesbury, one of England's greatest narrative historians, and regarded by some – me included – as the greatest between Bede (in the eighth century) and David Hume (in the eighteenth). Benedictine monk though William was, he was very far from being hostile to all worldly values; he appreciated art, architecture, commerce and urban life. Although shocked by the king's indifference to religion and tolerance of Judaism, his Rufus (not a name he ever used) was a man of many outstanding qualities. He was, in William's words, 'naturally gifted with a spirit prolific with great ideas'.[10] In his *History of the English Kings,* a book ranging from the fifth century to the early twelfth, and dealing with kings such as Alfred the Great, Athelstan, Cnut, William the Conqueror and Henry I, Rufus was the only one whom William likened to Alexander the Great and Julius Caesar. The king's generous treatment of enemies led William to make these comparisons, writing in the latter case that 'If our Christian faith permitted such an idea, it was as if the soul of Julius Caesar had migrated into King William.'[11]

In the light of the recent suggestion that William of Malmesbury may have been born *c.*1085, it is possible that while a boy he may have seen the king and heard him speak: 'he stammered when his temper began to rise'. It is to William that we owe the only surviving description of Rufus's appearance:

he was squarely built, with a ruddy complexion, light blond hair swept back so as to leave his forehead clear, his sparkling eyes speckled with gleaming flecks, physically strong despite his modest height, but somewhat paunchy ... In public and in assemblies his bearing was haughty and stiff. He would stare at people with a menacing look in his eyes, and intimidate those he was speaking to by adopting a harsh tone and a studied severity. In private and in the chamber with his friends he was easy-going, and relied a great deal on joking. He was in particular a most eloquent critic of his own mistakes, ensuring thereby that any resentment at what he had done dissolved into laughter.[12]

A king who liked to disarm criticism with a joke rather appealed to William, a historian whose own desire to amuse his readers was destined to offend serious-minded Victorian scholars. His portrait of Rufus has to be taken seriously, partly because he had good contacts at the royal court and partly because, caught between Eadmer's view and his own high estimate of his own judgement, his opinion of the king was an extraordinarily conflicted one. In one place he wrote that over time Rufus degenerated: his generosity became extravagance, his high-mindedness became pride and his firmness cruelty; in another that 'he would have been a prince without peer in our own time had he not been over-shadowed by his father and had not fate overtaken him at an early age, thus preventing the faults occasioned by unlimited power and youthful spirits from being corrected by maturity'.[13] On the subject of Rufus's character the master of Latin prose on one occasion expressed himself in so convoluted a fashion that where, on the evidence of all the manuscripts, he wrote 'undeservedly' (*immerito*), the best modern edition prefers the translation 'thoroughly deserved'.[14]

In recent times historians have tended to take a more tolerant view of the sins with which Rufus was charged. The process began with Frank Barlow's biography, *William Rufus*, published in 1983, and was taken significantly further by Emma Mason's *William II* (2005). Even so, to an astonishing extent modern historians have accepted the notion that Rufus was at fault in opposing 'reform'. Yet it can be argued that if he had given the religious radicals their head in their campaign to impose celibacy on the clergy, very many of whom had wives and children, the outcome would have been widespread turmoil and unhappiness. Many families throughout his dominions had reason to be grateful to a king who opposed this sort of 'reform'. In the event, however, it was precisely his attitude to 'reform' which, combined with his sudden death, shaped the prevailing image. The descriptions of Rufus's policies, lifestyle and values by ecclesiastical historians writing for posterity are the ones that would be repeated down the centuries, even by historians as independent-minded as Samuel Daniel in the seventeenth century and as sceptical of religion as David Hume in the eighteenth. In the most detailed of all studies of Rufus, the Victorian historian Edward Freeman concluded that the king's death 'set England free from oppression such as she never felt before or after at the hand of a single man', a ruler who 'stands well nigh alone in bringing back the foulest vices of heathendom into a Christian land'.[15] By the second half of the twentieth century this perception of Rufus was so entrenched that a respected Oxford historian was moved to write: 'From the moral standpoint he was probably the worst king that has occupied the throne of England.'[16] A king such as Rufus, accused of having sex without ever marrying, was evidently nastier than one who killed two of his six wives.

2
Taking the Throne

No record survives of Rufus's birth. The conventional date, *c.*1058, is derived from the statement that he was over forty years old when he died. As a king's son, even while still just a child, he was occasionally named as a witness in charters issued by his parents. Such formalities apart, the earliest reference to him in a contemporary narrative is in the *Anglo-Saxon Chronicle*'s annal for 1079:

> King William fought against his son Robert near a castle called Gerberoi, and King William was wounded there, and the horse he rode was killed. His son William was wounded there too, and many men were killed.

These few words with which Rufus made his entry into history reveal a great deal about the politics of power. In eleventh-century Europe, kingdoms, like other landed estates, were family firms and, as in modern family businesses, there was no fixed order of succession. At any time a struggle for control could pit brother against brother, nephew against uncle or, as here, son against father. Victory brought massive rewards. We know from Domesday Book (1086) that the winner in this game of thrones got no less than 20 per cent of all the land in England.

Struggles for wealth on this scale were fought by all means possible, including war. Kings and princes, despite being relatively well protected by high-quality body armour, risked being killed. As king, Rufus contributed to the emergence of a code of chivalry which meant, for example, that defeated leaders had a good chance of being allowed to live, as King Stephen would be after his capture at the Battle of Lincoln in 1141. But in 1079 there was as yet little sign of this new morality of war. On 14 October 1066 King Harold and two of his brothers had been among the many hundreds slaughtered at Hastings; the previous month another brother, Tostig, had been killed in the Battle of Stamford Bridge together with the King of Norway. Kings and princes were always prime targets, and not just in wars against external enemies. In the struggle for power that followed the killing of King Malcolm of Scotland and his son Edward in 1093, another of his sons, Duncan, was killed and his brother Donald Ban blinded. At Gerberoi in 1079 both young William and his father the Conqueror were relatively lucky. But despite the dangers to themselves, rulers and would-be rulers were expected to share the risks when they sent their followers to fight, not stay behind their desks as rulers do today. For as long as this expectation prevailed, it was virtually impossible for women to become monarchs. William the Conqueror's seal portrayed him as a warrior on horseback, and so did William II's.

Given the dangers a young prince was going to face, it is anything but surprising that training for war figured largely in his education. Rufus was, wrote William of Malmesbury, 'raised with the greatest care by his parents'. His mother, Queen Matilda, presumably supervised his upbringing as a child. Then he entered a male-dominated world.

> Once his childhood was over, he spent his youth in military exercises: horsemanship and weapon training. He competed against those older than himself with due deference, and with ceremonial respect against those of his own age. He thought less of himself if he were not the first to issue a challenge to a fight, or hit back at anyone who challenged him.[1]

The adult Rufus was portrayed as occasionally acting impetuously. A rash solo attack against a body of enemy cavalry in 1091 nearly ended in his death when his horse was killed under him. He was dragged along the ground by his foot, and William of Malmesbury believed that only his hauberk saved him from being seriously hurt. Yet no sooner had another charger been brought to him than he leaped onto it without waiting for a mounting block.[2] Some of the skills involved in riding to war could be effectively acquired by learning to hunt. Alfred the Great's mastery of 'the whole art of hunting' was one of the attributes which led to him being regarded as a model ruler.[3] Hunting, like war, was dangerous. One of Rufus's older brothers, Richard, died as a result of injuries suffered while hunting in the New Forest. In consequence Rufus became the second oldest of the three surviving brothers: Robert, William, Henry. Their rivalry was to shape the politics of a generation.

As adolescents both Rufus and Henry were attached to

the household of Archbishop Lanfranc of Canterbury. Both were knighted by Lanfranc, Henry as an eighteen-year-old in 1086, Rufus at unknown date, but presumably by 1079 since the ceremony marked his coming of age as an adult fighting man. Orderic described Henry's knighting: 'Lanfranc dressed him in a hauberk, placed a helmet on his head, and girded him in the name of the Lord with the belt of knighthood.'[4] Prelates, like all lords, expected to be escorted by knights and were required to send military contingents to war. But in aristocratic households young men were trained for more than war. They were expected to acquire manners and learn to value good service by performing it themselves. A contemporary list of seven knightly accomplishments included swimming, falconry, song-writing and the newly fashionable game of chess, as well as riding, archery and combat. Although Lanfranc's learning led William of Malmesbury to write that he 'inspired the whole Latin world to pursue the liberal arts',[5] there is nothing to indicate that Rufus learned to read or write – unlike Henry, who did, whether because he had originally been intended for the priesthood, or because he was ten years younger than Rufus, in a world of changing expectations. By the 1120s the saying 'an illiterate king is an ass wearing a crown' had become proverbial.[6]

Another episode involving Rufus occurred before the battle at Gerberoi, but we know about it only from a story told by Orderic some fifty years later. Rufus and Henry were in the upper gallery of a house in Laigle (Normandy) playing a noisy game of dice 'as soldiers do', when they added to their fun by pissing down over Robert and his friends in the hall below. Bedlam ensued when Robert raced upstairs to punish them, and their father had to be summoned. According to Orderic, this was fierce sibling rivalry, not just high spirits: 'William and Henry thought it shameful that Robert aspired to the whole inheritance and thought himself the equal of his father.' The terms on which the king restored order at Laigle left Robert deeply dissatisfied. 'Next night he and his followers hurried to Rouen, where they tried to capture the citadel by stealth.'[7] When this attempted coup misfired, they fled. Robert made common cause with his father's enemies, notably King Philip of France. From him he acquired the castle of Gerberoi in the Beauvaisis as a base from which he and his followers, young men with high hopes of prospering when the next generation took over, launched the raids into Normandy that provoked King William into laying siege to the castle in 1079.

By this date father-to-son succession to the throne had been accepted as the norm in England and France. But it was not a foregone conclusion that sons would succeed in order of seniority, especially when, as in this case, the father ruled over two distinct polities. Robert, some five years older than Rufus, and from an early age publicly recognized as the heir to Normandy, was in a strong position to succeed in England too. His father's policy of giving lands confiscated from English rebels to Frenchmen, chiefly Normans, had created a single cross-Channel aristocracy, men possessing great estates on both sides of the sea. For them life was relatively simple while one man ruled both Normandy and England. But if the Conqueror's empire were divided, they would have to serve two masters and run the risk of losing estates on one side or the other when the two fell out. In 1079 there was no obvious reason to believe that Robert would not mature into a competent ruler. As one of the leaders of the First Crusade he was to win the reputation of being a great warrior.

But in the late 1070s relations between him and his father were tense. No doubt he wanted the share in the government of Normandy to which he felt entitled, but the king was unwilling to relinquish any of his power. According to John of Worcester, using a now lost version of the *Anglo-Saxon Chronicle*, it was Robert himself who wounded and unhorsed King William at Gerberoi. By contrast Rufus, in William of Malmesbury's words, 'was always obedient. In battle he displayed his prowess in his father's sight, and in peace he walked at his side.'[8] It was a familiar story. While the eldest son chafed at the bit, his younger brother displayed conspicuous loyalty. But in 1079 relations between King William and Robert were not yet fatally damaged. At Gerberoi Robert killed the king's horse, but the moment he heard his father's voice and realized who it was, he dismounted and gave him his own horse. Not much later they were reconciled, perhaps at the queen's prompting. Her death in November 1083 deprived the family of its best-placed peacemaker. Even so, it may not have been until 1087 that Robert once again turned against his father and joined forces with King Philip of France.

The huge increase in power which Duke William of Normandy obtained as a consequence of the conquest of England unnerved all his neighbours, especially the King of France. Despite being acknowledged as the overlord of the kingdom as a whole, in practice the French king had little power outside the Île de France (the region around Paris). Dukes of Normandy, like other French princes such as the counts of Flanders, Anjou, Poitou and Toulouse, held sovereign jurisdictional authority within their own principalities. They minted their own coins and retained effective power of patronage and appointment within their borders. But few land borders were clearly drawn; aristocratic families commonly held land on both sides. Frontiers were zones of turbulence, none more so than the Vexin, a region in the Seine valley between Paris and Rouen, and the scene of many of the conflicts in which King William I continued to take an active part – even though in his late fifties he grew so fat as to become the butt of King Philip's jokes. It was in the Vexin in July 1087, as the Normans fought their way into and torched the town of Mantes, that the Conqueror was brought down by a combination of exhaustion, the heat of the conflagration and internal injury inflicted when his horse stumbled in the mêlée.

When it became obvious that he was dying, his two youngest sons were summoned to his bedside, but not Robert. According to a pamphlet commissioned by Rufus to set out his right to the throne, the dying king had been so troubled by the prospect of his realm slipping into chaos if he were succeeded by his first-born son that he named William as his heir, and handed the regalia, crown, sword and sceptre over to him. To some of the most influential people at the king's side, however, notably his half-brother, Count Robert of Mortain, and Archbishop John of Rouen, it did not seem right that Robert should be disinherited.

Reluctantly the king gave in to their group pressure. 'Since he has disdained to come here himself, it is with you as witnesses that I act now. I forgive him all the sins he has committed against me, and I grant him the whole duchy of Normandy.'[9]

What this account of William I's deathbed doesn't say is that Rufus didn't stay to the end. He was in a hurry to get to England. In the minds of many he was trying to steal the throne, and unless he moved fast, he would lose his chance. His father understood. He gave him a letter addressed to Archbishop Lanfranc and told him to leave at once. At the Norman coast Rufus paused, waiting for definite news before embarking. When William the Conqueror died, of his sons only Henry, to whom the king had bequeathed a fortune in cash, was in attendance. Orderic, who never knowingly missed an opportunity to moralize about the vanity of earthly glory, described the chaotic scene in Rouen when the old king died and Henry rushed away to get his treasure, followed by another darkly farcical one at the burial in Caen. When they tried to push William's bloated body into the stone sarcophagus, it burst, filling the church with a foul smell.[10] No Anselm he.

By then Rufus was in England. He headed first for Winchester. Control of this city, the old West Saxon centre with a royal treasury and depository for fiscal records, had been recognized as the key to power since the 1040s. According to William of Malmesbury, he was 'welcomed by the inhabitants and secured the key of the royal treasure'. His next step was to see his old mentor. According to Eadmer, in order to overcome Lanfranc's doubts about his suitability,

Rufus promised him that he would maintain justice, mercy and equity and defend the Church against all its enemies, but no sooner was he firmly on the throne than he began go back on his promises. When Lanfranc gently chided him, Rufus responded angrily: 'Who can keep all his promises?'[11] This marks the opening shot in Eadmer's campaign to present Rufus as an unscrupulous tyrant – though the promises described as specific to Rufus were standard features of the coronation oath sworn by all kings. Another Canterbury source merely observed that 'Lanfranc chose his son William as king, just as his father had wanted'.[12] Royal successions were normally disputed and the outcome decided by politics and war; in that sense the successful claimant was the one chosen by the people. Nonetheless the previous king's last will was widely regarded as creating an acceptable title.

On Sunday 26 September, seventeen days after his father died, Rufus was anointed and crowned by the Archbishop of Canterbury in Westminster Abbey, built only twenty years earlier but already the location of two previous coronations, those of Harold II and William I. All present swore allegiance. Now formally king, Rufus returned to Winchester. Possession of his father's great store of wealth would be a potentially decisive advantage in the forthcoming struggle against Robert. According to the *Anglo-Saxon Chronicle*:

> it was impossible for anyone to describe how much gold and silver was accumulated there, how many costly robes and jewels, as well as many other precious objects that it is difficult to list.

Rufus at once put this to good political use, by doing as his father had asked. To secure prayers for his father's soul he distributed alms on a lavish scale: to each minster church in England either six or ten marks (four or 6.66 pounds) of gold; to each parish church 60d; to every shire £100 to be distributed to the poor. Battle Abbey, founded by his father in penance for that great slaughter, got even more, including a manor worth £40 per annum, 300 gold and silver reliquaries and a royal mantle adorned with gold and jewels. This grand gesture of filial piety and of devotion to God met with general approval.

In one respect only did Rufus go against his father's instructions. The dying man had asked that prisoners should be released, but Rufus freed neither Wulfnoth, King Harold's only surviving brother, nor Morcar, the last English earl of Northumbria. Although there had been no violent resistance to the Norman regime since 1080, no one could be sure that the war of English independence would not be renewed. By keeping Wulfnoth and Morcar in custody in Winchester, Rufus followed his father's practice rather than his dying wish. According to Orderic, King William I had said that he would like England to go to his son William, but did not dare to transmit to anyone a kingdom he had seized by mass murder, so he entrusted it to God. Rufus had a seal cut to an appropriate new design, bearing the words *dei gracia rex Anglorum* (by God's grace king of the English). He was the first king of England to take this style.

Towards Robert, who had been readily accepted as duke in Normandy, Rufus adopted a conciliatory policy. As a signal of his wish to avoid a war of succession, he restored his uncle Odo, Robert's most influential counsellor, to all his estates in England. Odo, made Bishop of Bayeux while still in his teens, had been William I's right-hand man during and after 1066. He had been rewarded by being made Earl of Kent and the king's richest subject, but by 1082 his relentless ambition – it was said that he aimed to be pope – so disconcerted the Conqueror that he had him arrested. When Odo claimed immunity on the grounds that he was a bishop, Lanfranc told him that he was being arrested as an earl. Not until 1087 when William I was dying did he, under pressure from Robert of Mortain (Odo's brother), agree to release him.

Shortly after Easter (16 April 1088) it became clear that Rufus's calculated generosity had misfired.

> The country was greatly disturbed and filled with much treachery, as the most powerful Frenchmen in the land planned to betray their lord the king and have his brother Robert as king. At the head of this plot was Bishop Odo.[13]

This was not just the English chronicler giving vent to his prejudice. All the greatest landowners in England were French and only three of Domesday's 'top ten', Earl Hugh of Chester, Alan of Richmond and William de Warenne, are known to have supported Rufus. Ominously the plotters included four of his father's closest counsellors. Odo, Robert of Mortain and their cousin Roger Montgomery, Earl of Shrewsbury, were the top three in the Domesday rich list; the fourth, Geoffrey Mowbray, Bishop of Coutances, was an experienced army commander – he knew, it was said, 'more about teaching soldiers to fight than clerks to sing psalms'[14] – and was also in the top ten. Revolts broke out more or less simultaneously in several regions where these men and their allies had followers ready to fight for them: the south-east, East Anglia, the Midlands, the north and the West Country. The timetable implies a degree of co-ordination, which suggests that the leading rebels had met together, perhaps at the king's Easter court.

The rebels fortified their castles and ravaged and plundered the lands of those who had not yet joined them. From his base within the Roman walls of Rochester Odo devastated Lanfranc's estates and threatened London. Earl Roger did not immediately show his hand, but three of his sons joined Odo. The eldest, Robert of Bellême, was already a famous soldier. Orderic, who hated him, described him as 'a man of keen intelligence, treacherous and devious, strong and well-built, bold and powerful in war, ready in speech, appallingly cruel, prepared to endure unremitting toil, a master builder of castles and siege machines and a torturer of human beings'.[15] In Normandy, Henry decided to support Robert, handing him, in return for a grant of rights over the Cotentin and Avranchin, the treasure that had been his legacy. Robert sent a force under the command of Eustace of Boulogne, also in the 'top ten', to Rochester. With other landing places such as Chichester harbour and Arundel (held by Earl Roger), Pevensey (held by Robert of Mortain) and Hastings (held by another major landowner, William of Eu) in rebel hands, all that remained was for Robert to cross the Channel. Good judges have thought it amazing that Rufus survived.

Things got worse when Rufus's principal counsellor, Bishop William of Durham, left court without permission. On 12 May the king gave orders for his arrest, but he escaped to the safety of Durham Castle, from where he wrote to the king, denying that he had done anything wrong and blaming his enemies for poisoning the king's mind against him – signs of an atmosphere of tension and suspicion at court. The author of the *Anglo-Saxon Chronicle* was not convinced, writing that the bishop treated the king 'just as Judas Iscariot did our Lord'. Conscious of the potential of native sentiment, Rufus harnessed it to prop up his tottering regime. He

> sent for Englishmen and explained his need to them. He begged for their support, promising them the best law there had ever been in this country, forbidding unjust taxes and granting men their hunting rights. It did not last for long, but nonetheless the English came to the aid of the king their lord.[16]

In this crisis, with so many of the magnates against him, he owed much to the predominantly English shire levies under the sheriffs' command.

Rufus concentrated on the south-east, where Duke Robert might come, leaving local forces to deal with rebels in their area. In Worcestershire the English bishop co-operated with the Norman sheriff to defeat an army from Shropshire and Herefordshire (presumably Earl Roger's tenants). The king's own first priority was to secure London, making it his central supply depot, and arranging for ships to blockade Pevensey and Rochester. Then he headed for Rochester. His target was Odo. At Tonbridge Castle, which he captured after a two-day siege, he learned that Odo had left Rochester and gone to Pevensey, perhaps to stiffen the resolve of his brother. Rufus immediately headed south. Pevensey Castle, protected by the sea as well as by strong walls, held out for six weeks against his siege machines. During those weeks rebels elsewhere were on the rampage, but Rufus was not to be deflected. The crucial turning point came when a fleet sent by Duke Robert was intercepted by English ships, and in the ensuing naval battle suffered heavy losses. Soon after that the defenders of Pevensey ran out of provisions and negotiated terms of surrender. In return for being allowed to leave England, Odo promised to persuade the rebels in Rochester to surrender, and was sent ahead under escort in order to carry this out.

On arrival at Rochester, however, Odo and his escort were 'captured' in a sally by the defenders. The revolt continued. There were few who did not think Odo had connived at this, and when Rufus arrived with the main army he was understandably furious. In hindsight he had been too generous, but it has to be remembered that only the English thought of the rebels as out-and-out traitors: in Norman eyes they were men making hard choices in an awkward situation. In the aftermath of his victory at Pevensey Rufus's conciliatory policy persuaded many of those who had previously opted for Robert that they had little to fear if they now changed sides. After all, as Rufus said to Earl Roger in a conversation reported, or imagined, by William of Malmesbury:

If you think my father was wrong about me, what does this say about you and your fellows? The same man who made me king made you great lords.[17]

Only those who still held out in Rochester did not accept this political logic.

Rufus pressed the siege vigorously. His artillery destroyed the castle (a timber one) and damaged cathedral property. But his best weapon was hunger and disease in the over-crowded city. In the summer heat so many flies bred in the rotting corpses of men and horses that it became impossible for anyone to eat anything unless someone else stood by beating the flies away. Presumably Odo and his friends continued to hope that, if they held out long enough, Duke Robert would land. But he never came. Eventually the rebels could bear the miseries of the siege no longer, and they negotiated terms of surrender. Orderic believed that opinion in the king's army was divided, the English wanting to see the rebels hanged as traitors, the Normans, at their head Earl Roger, pleading for clemency for men who were, after all, friends and family. Again Rufus decided to show mercy. The rebels, Earl Roger's sons among them, were allowed to leave with their horses and arms – though Odo's request that the king's trumpeters should not sound, as was customary when a stronghold was taken by force, was rejected. Some, such as Gilbert de Clare of Tonbridge and Geoffrey of Coutances, were allowed to submit and keep their estates. Others had their estates confiscated, principally Odo, Eustace of Boulogne, Robert of Bellême and William of Eu. But Rufus did not grant their lands to others, allowing them to hope that by serving the king well in the future they might recover them. For all except one this was a real possibility. Odo's desperate gamble had ensured that Rufus would never again trust him. 'The magnanimous king', as Orderic calls him here,

> deliberately turned a blind eye to the guilt of some ... Consequently some of those who had gone furthest in their treachery obeyed him with even greater devotion in the years that followed, endeavouring to get into his good books with gifts, flattery and service.[18]

Hoping to take advantage of his brother's policy, Henry came to England, asking that the lands which had once belonged to their mother should now be given to him. But in Rufus's eyes Henry had done nothing that deserved rewarding, and he gave those estates to someone who did, his steward, Robert fitz Haimo, son of the Sheriff of Kent. There was some tidying-up to be done. The church of Rochester was compensated for the damage it suffered during the siege, and Bishop Gundulf was set to work building a stone castle, much of which is still standing today.

All that remained was to deal with Rufus's 'Judas Iscariot', Bishop William of Durham, safe but immobilized in Durham Castle. The devastation of his church's estates by the Sheriff of York brought him to negotiate. He came to court under safe conduct, but refused to accept that he could be put on trial like a layman. He was allowed to return to Durham. In September three northern magnates, Alan of Richmond, Roger Montgomery, lord of Lancaster, and Odo of Champagne, lord of Holderness, persuaded the bishop to come to court again, this time promising that if he did not accept the court's decision then the king would provide him with ships and crews at a south-coast port so that he could accept exile with honour. On 2 November 1088 the trial began at Salisbury (now Old Sarum). An account composed only a few years later is notable for its reportage of the cut and thrust of argument between the bishop and Lanfranc and of the uproar among the laity provoked by the bishop's demand for ecclesiastical privilege – his right not to be tried in a secular court and his right of appeal to the papal curia. To which Lanfranc, supported by the other bishops present, replied: 'We are not judging you as bishop but as the holder of great estate.' Bishop William would not give ground. But this time the king refused to release him until Durham Castle had been surrendered. 'You can talk as much as you like,' said the king, 'but you will not be freed until your castle has been handed over. The bishop of Bayeux caused me no end of trouble because I trusted his word. See to it that my men have possession of Durham castle by 14 November and you will get your safe-conduct and your ships.'[19] Next month the bishop and his entourage were allowed to sail to Normandy.

How had Rufus pulled off this victory against the odds? Two factors were vital. The first was Duke Robert's failure to put in an appearance during the months of May, June and July – too long a period to be explained by unfavourable wind direction. This failure remains a puzzle. Implicitly Orderic explained it by portraying him as a lazy and lascivious man who was weak and ineffectual in all things. But on crusade Robert was neither weak nor lazy. Orderic's portrait of him reflected his determination to excuse Henry I's later treatment of his brother (whom he attacked, captured and held in prison for life). One possible explanation is that, from Robert's point of view, England did not matter quite as much as another territory, and one closer to home, which was also slipping from his grasp – Maine. Formally he was Count of Maine as well as Duke of Normandy, but Norman control of Maine was opposed by many Manceaux and it is possible that for him trying to hold on to Maine was a higher priority than fighting his brother over England. The second crucial factor was Rufus himself: his determination, his conduct of siege warfare, including his use of naval forces to blockade and intercept, and finally his strategic sense, both politically – his shrewdly judged leniency – and militarily, his unswerving focus on Odo and the south-east.

3
The English Church

Then the venerable father Lanfranc died and William oppressed all the churches and monasteries of England most harshly.[1]

Eadmer's narrative of Rufus's reign in his *Vita Anselmi* begins with these plain and immensely influential words. But in plain fact not all churches felt oppressed. The monks of Durham had been worried that, with their bishop in exile, they might be vulnerable, but

when the prior went to the king, he rose humbly and received him kindly. He not only took nothing from them but made them gifts from his own resources, protecting them from the attacks of ill-wishers just as his father had done. It was during this period that our present refectory was built.[2]

Rufus's reign witnessed the launch of Durham's spectacular building plans. At Battle Abbey, he was remembered as

the magnificent prince who endowed us with churches in Suffolk, Norfolk and Essex ... So much did he love, cherish and defend our church, maintaining its dignity and royal customs, that no one would dare oppose it, just as no one had dared do so in his father's time. Whenever he was in the neighbourhood, he would often visit, support and encourage it, so great was his affection for it.[3]

He helped to found Bermondsey Priory by providing the land on which it was built. The monastic order as a whole flourished during his reign. Between 1086 (Domesday Book) and 1100 no fewer than twenty-six new Benedictine and six new Cluniac houses were founded.

But Eadmer's was far from being a lone voice. After Rufus's death, the author of the *Anglo-Saxon Chronicle*'s judgement was severe:

> He oppressed God's church, and all the bishoprics and abbacies whose incumbents died he either sold for money or retained in his own hands and rented out ... and so on the day he died he had in his own hands the archbishopric of Canterbury, the bishoprics of Winchester and Salisbury, as well as eleven abbacies which had been rented out.

Henry I exploited this widely held view in the charter he issued on 5 August 1100, three days after Rufus died. 'Because the realm has been oppressed by unjust exactions, I first of all make the Church free.'

But in August 1100 the Archbishop of Canterbury was not dead but abroad, and had been for nearly three years. For this the English Church had paid a price. Its leader's absence made it much harder to fill ecclesiastical posts as they became vacant, exacerbating precisely the problem complained about most. Why then had Anselm left? Years later Eadmer summed up his own account of this by saying that the king drove him out of the kingdom. But Eadmer's narrative is a tissue of half-truths and omissions. In fact Anselm had not been condemned to exile – as Bishop William of Durham had been in 1088 – nor had he been forced to flee abroad as Becket would be in 1164. In 1097 he had pestered the king to let him go until in the end Rufus gave way. In the strikingly neutral words of the *Anglo-Saxon Chronicle*, 'With the king's reluctant permission, Anselm went overseas because *it seemed to him* [my italics] that in this country little was done according to justice and according to his orders.'[4] It took the unanswerable judgment of God to persuade this anonymous monk to come out strongly in Anselm's favour, writing in his entry for 1100 of 'the great injustice which King William did him'.

Anselm himself explained how he felt and why he wanted to resign in a letter he sent to Pope Urban soon after leaving England in late 1097:

I have been archbishop for four fruitless years, living uselessly and in immense and horrible tribulation to my soul, so that now every day I would rather die outside England than continue to live there. If I were to die there in the condition I was in, my soul would be damned, for in that land I saw many evils which I ought not to have tolerated, but was unable to correct as a bishop should. The king treated churches badly after the deaths of their prelates. He harassed me and the church of Canterbury in many ways ... refusing to restore those estates he had given to his knights while they were in his hands after Lanfranc's death. Indeed against my

35

wishes he gave away others as it suited him. From me he required unprecedentedly heavy services, more than I should rightly suffer. At the same time I saw the laws of God and canonical and apostolic authority flouted by arbitrary impositions. When I spoke out about all these things, I achieved nothing. Knowing therefore that if I were to continue in this way, I would in effect confirm these wicked practices to the detriment of my successors and to the damnation of my soul ... and finding that I could find no support – for no one dared advise or help me in this – I asked the king's permission to approach you to disclose the distress of my heart to you and confer with you about what might be most salutary for my soul.[5]

One of the striking things about this letter – apart from Anselm's obsessive anxiety about the state of his own soul – is the fact that 'apostolic authority' was mentioned only in passing. There is nothing here to suggest that, as Eadmer claimed, Rufus had given Anselm an ultimatum: either he must promise never to appeal to the pope on any matter whatever or leave the country at once.[6] Anselm's own emphasis was on Rufus's treatment of Canterbury's material resources, on unspecified 'evils' and on his own inability to improve things. Two years later when he wrote to Urban's successor, Paschal II, in autumn 1099, he still wanted to resign, but he now played some new notes:

The king would not allow the pope to be recognized in England unless he commanded it, nor was I permitted to write a letter to the pope, or receive one from him, or obey his decrees. Not once since the beginning of his reign has he allowed a council to be held.[7]

At Easter 1099 Anselm had attended Urban's council at Rome and witnessed papal leadership of the Church in action, hearing the pope issue decrees banning lay investiture and excommunicating all clerics who did homage to laymen. Yet in 1093 Anselm had done homage to Rufus, and even later he remained relaxed about using phrases such as 'the king gave me this archbishopric'.[8] Only after Easter 1099 did Anselm write about the issues at stake in that great conflict between State and Church known as the Investiture Contest. Had Anselm wanted to fight for papal authority in the 1090s, he might have helped Walter of Albano, papal legate to England in 1095, hold a reform council, but to Walter's displeasure he had refused to do so. In his policy towards the papacy Rufus had been following in his father's footsteps; and although his father had allowed Lanfranc to hold councils, in William of Malmesbury's judgement, 'in council nothing could be done except what he dictated'. Although Eadmer liked to represent the relationship between William I and Lanfranc as a harmonious ideal, this is not how William of Malmesbury thought it had been:

The king was arrogant beyond measure and often did things for no good reason but simply because he possessed immense power. Not only did he use violence to enforce his will in secular matters, but he intervened entirely improperly in Church matters . . . Money was needed to counter the attacks of enemies and he seized it . . . The archbishop put up with all this because he had no choice; weighed down as he was by the king's extraordinary arrogance, he could not stand up against his vices. But he studied his character, chose time and place, making quiet interventions and well-timed suggestions, chipping away at some things, moderating the impact of others.[9]

Lanfranc stayed in post until his death, nineteen years in all. After four years Anselm wanted to resign. No one wanted him to go. Even in Eadmer's version both the king and the other bishops begged him to stay. Bishop Walklin of Winchester said: 'it is hard to believe that you will insist on throwing away the dignity and opportunities for good which the exalted position of archbishop affords'.[10] But he did insist, and went. The king's agents moved in and took possession of Canterbury's property, leaving the monks with only enough, as Anselm complained to the pope, for their food and clothing – doubtless rather hard on monks accustomed to greater comfort.

Had Anselm stayed in England in 1097, he would no doubt have had a hard time of it. Rufus saw himself as the master of the churches in England, as his father had and as his younger brother would. Throughout Christian Europe churches owed their existence to the piety and generosity of those wealthy landowners, usually laymen, who had endowed them; hardly surprising, then, that kings and secular lords selected the bishops, abbots and priests who headed 'their' churches. The major churches were immensely rich. Approximately one-quarter of the wealth of all

England as measured in Domesday Book belonged to them. Kings expected something in return – sometimes a substantial cash payment or, at the very least, reliable political and military support – from the prelates they appointed. As outward signs of this relationship they required them to swear fidelity to them and do homage. During intervals between the deaths of prelates and the installation of new ones, kings' agents managed 'vacant' churches and, after making an allowance for monks or canons, kept the lion's share of its revenues for their masters. Two bishoprics were vacant when Rufus fell dangerously ill in 1093. Lincoln had been vacant for almost a year. That was defensible, but Canterbury was still vacant nearly four years after Lanfranc's death in May 1089. On what he thought was his deathbed, Rufus filled both. He chose his chancellor, Robert Bloet, as Bishop of Lincoln. As successor to Canterbury's scholar-monk, Lanfranc, formerly Abbot of Bec, he chose an even greater theologian, Anselm, also Abbot of Bec.

But then Rufus recovered. King and archbishop were soon at odds. What they argued about was the amount of help that Anselm would give. As an investment on which he expected a good return, Robert Bloet had been willing to pay £5,000 for his bishopric. Henry of Huntingdon remembered being in Bishop Robert's household: 'the handsome knights, noble young men, expensive horses, his golden and gilt dishes, the number of courses, the splendour of his servants, the purple garments and the satins'.[11] Anselm offered only a tenth of that for the richer see of Canterbury. When Rufus rejected this as derisory, he got nothing. At times they co-operated well enough, but when they did not, as when Anselm demanded the restoration of those Canterbury estates, it was a tussle between king and archbishop over the privileges and material resources of the church of Canterbury. In 1097 Anselm found himself under attack for the allegedly poor quality of the troops which his church had provided for a campaign in Wales, and he decided he had had enough. He wanted to think and write theology. It was understandable, but hardly heroic.

In self-imposed exile Anselm became sharply aware of an intoxicating idea which a generation earlier had won powerful adherents in Rome but which, in a world of intermittent and slow communications, had as yet hardly impinged on northern Europe. The Church should be free. The secular world should be kept out of Church business. Holders of ecclesiastical office, those responsible for looking after men's souls, should be 'freely' chosen by other churchmen, not by secular lords who inevitably preferred and selected the kinds of men that suited their interests, political as much as religious. Kings, wrote the militant Pope Gregory VII (1073–85), after whom the movement has been labelled the 'Gregorian Reform', 'are people who, prompted by the devil, strive to dominate through treachery, murder, arrogance, plunder'.[12] Not surprisingly, such ideas were highly controversial, especially since they went hand in hand with the conviction that churchmen should be free from other secular ties. They should be 'pure', they should refrain from sex (both in and out of marriage), from hunting, bearing arms and gambling; in matters of dress and hairstyle they were to follow strict rules. These radical demands had divided the Church. There were two popes. In Normandy Duke Robert recognized Urban as pope, but Rufus continued the policy his father and Lanfranc had adopted since 1085 by recognizing neither of them.

Yet some of the fundamentalists' ideas were catching on. In 1091 Abbot Herbert of Ramsey offered £1,000 and was made Bishop of East Anglia, but later decided that he had sinned, and sought absolution from Urban. When he returned, Rufus deprived him of the bishopric at an assembly of bishops and magnates which convened at Hastings in February 1094. Eadmer composed a long account of the assembly focusing on Anselm's determination to insist on Canterbury's authority over other bishops and on his wish to hold a council. It included a lively dialogue between archbishop and king in which Rufus was portrayed as uninterested in stamping out sodomy. At this point in his narrative Eadmer inserted a description of effeminate fashions at court (see p. 50). But there was not a word about Rufus's treatment of Bishop Herbert, so fixated was Eadmer on Anselm.

Seen in the hindsight of 1099, it was plain to Eadmer that Anselm had all along been engaged in a heroic struggle for the freedom of the Church. He interpreted the notes he had made of his archbishop's quarrels with Rufus, exaggerating the extent to which principled ideas about the 'liberty of the Church' were an issue. His great set piece was a confrontation between the archbishop and the king's spokesmen over the issue of royal against papal authority at a meeting of the council at Rockingham in 1095. Accused of undermining the king's sovereignty by claiming the right to visit Urban, Anselm appealed from the king's court to the pope's.

> At that moment they understood what had previously never occurred to them, that in Anselm's view an archbishop of Canterbury could not be forced to answer to any man on any charge whatever except to the pope.[13]

Given the fact that the king's chief spokesman at Rockingham was none other than the Bishop of Durham, now back in royal favour, who in 1088 had wanted to appeal to the pope on the grounds that as an ecclesiastic he could not be judged in a secular court (an argument scornfully dismissed by Lanfranc), it seems unlikely that Anselm's appeal in 1095 caused much of a stir – which may be why no contemporary source so much as mentions the Council of Rockingham.

Rufus had in fact already asked Urban to send a legate to England. He wanted the prelates of Normandy on his side in his campaign to oust Robert, so it clearly made political sense to recognize the pope they had already accepted. When Walter of Albano arrived he disappointed Rufus, according to Eadmer, by refusing to depose Anselm. Fortunately we have an alternative contemporary source of information in the chronicle composed by Hugh of Flavigny, a French monk and keen Gregorian, who visited England in 1096 in the entourage of a second papal legate. He strongly disapproved of the agreement that Walter and Rufus came to in 1095: no papal legate or letter would be received or obeyed in England except on the king's orders; Anselm promised fidelity to the pope 'saving the fealty he owed to the king'. Eadmer preferred not to mention this agreement, just as he omitted Anselm's obstruction of Walter's plan to hold a council. Even more strikingly, Eadmer chose not to mention the 1096 legation at all. The legate, Abbot Jarento of Dijon, intended to legislate in council against simony, clerical fornication and ecclesiastical vacancies. Rufus received him reverently and detained him honourably at court until, to the king's delight, a new envoy arrived from Urban, deferring consideration of these awkward matters to a later date. Hugh of Flavigny was annoyed at having to listen to the king's criticism of a pope who had dishonourably undermined the authority of his own legate by sending a message via 'a lowly lackey, some sort of nephew to the pope'. He was convinced that Urban had been influenced by a royal gift of ten marks (6.6 pounds) of pure gold.[14]

The Rufus who exacerbated disputes by flaring up angrily is a creation of Eadmer's pen, quite different from the Rufus described by Hugh of Flavigny, with his strategy of postponing awkward matters by courtesy and bribery. According to William of Malmesbury, the Conqueror had been in the habit of saying that well-timed gifts had the power to deflect all churchmen, from the pope downwards. Henry I would follow where his father and brother had led – except that he, unlike Rufus, did allow Anselm to hold a council, and when Anselm seized the opportunity to require married priests to put aside their wives, the king enforced the decree by methods which provoked a protest in London by some two hundred barefooted priests. Their demonstration reduced the queen to tears, but she was too frightened of her husband to intervene on their behalf. It is not necessarily obvious that a king who refused to grant Anselm permission to hold a council should be regarded as a reprobate opponent of reform rather than as the protector of the majority of his clergy and their families.

Rufus's complaints about Canterbury's military contingent in 1097 and his refusal to let Anselm hold his council led the archbishop to renew his request for permission to go to Rome. His fellow bishops advised him against defying the king's wishes. When asked to choose between the king and archbishop, they all chose, in Eadmer's words, 'to follow the will of an earthly man'.[15] Irrespective of how far Eadmer was using hindsight to tidy up the arguments used on both sides, it is significant that on this and many other occasions he presented Anselm as a lone voice upholding God and the liberty of the Church against everyone else, including all the other bishops. Evidently they all took a different view of the best interests of the Church. The four bishops who worked most closely with Rufus were Walklin of Winchester and his successor William Giffard, William of Durham and his successor, Ranulf Flambard. The great cathedrals of Winchester and Durham stand today as monuments to what these men could get done.

In financial terms Rufus pressed many churches very hard. Flambard, his principal financial adviser, acquired a great reputation for ruthless innovation – he may well have had a hand in the making of Domesday Book – and was often put in charge of vacant churches before being made Bishop of Durham in 1099 in return for an offer of £1,000. In August 1100 he paid a price for the unpopularity caused by his legendary ingenuity at screwing money out of the rich when Henry had him arrested and put in the Tower. It could not hold him for long. He got the jailers drunk, slid down from an upper storey using rope smuggled in inside a wine cask and escaped to Normandy. Henry later realized his usefulness and restored him to his see.

Far from Rufus having forced the archbishop to go into exile, he had left of his own accord, obstinately proclaiming that he obeyed only God's law. It was precisely at this juncture that Eadmer inserted into his narrative a number of anecdotes showing the world just how horrible Rufus was. It turned out that not only was he a demanding taskmaster for the church of Canterbury and a promoter of shockingly lax sexual morals, but he was also an unbeliever – or at least a sceptic – and a Jew-lover. Rufus, he wrote, used to assert that either God has no knowledge of men's actions or, if he does, does not weigh them properly. On one occasion fifty men were accused of poaching the king's deer, and were sent to trial by ordeal. As often happened when there was suspicion but no witnesses and – as usual in times before the age of forensic science – no compelling evidence either, it was reckoned that only God knew the truth. In this case the accused, after swearing their innocence, had to walk three paces carrying a lump of hot iron blessed by a priest. Three days later their hands were inspected and were seen to be healing well. In consequence, to the king's disappointment, they were declared innocent.

When the king was told of the verdict, he is said to have exclaimed in disgust: 'What! God a just judge! Let no one ever think so again! In the future, and this I swear, people will answer to my judgement, not to God's.'[16]

Eadmer's intention had been to besmirch Rufus's reputation – though if he had been sceptical of the ordeal as a means of getting at the truth, he would not have been alone. Indeed opinion against ordeals hardened during the twelfth century, and in 1215 the pope prohibited priests from taking part in them, a ban which effectively ended the practice, leading, in Britain, to trial by jury instead. But in fact Rufus was not opposed to ordeals in principle. A letter written by Ivo of Chartres reveals that Rufus had wanted to impose the ordeal by hot iron on the Bishop of Le Mans.

In another of Eadmer's anecdotes Rufus, in return for a fee, lent a sympathetic ear to a Jewish father's request that he restore his son, a recent convert to Christianity, to the religion of his fathers. Jews provided significant money-lending, money-changing and banking services, and they looked to rulers for protection and for assistance in collecting debts owed to them. 'My lord king, you must be joking' was, in this version, the son's reaction to Rufus's instruction that he revert to Judaism.

'Joking with you, you son of a shit heap? Do what I tell you at once, or by the holy face of Lucca, I'll have your eyes torn out!'[17]

But the young man was not to be moved by threats, and Rufus, put to shame – even in Eadmer's version – by the convert's courage, let him go free. The money-loving king still insisted on being paid for his effort, in the end taking half of the original fee. In other cases, however, by threats and intimidation Rufus succeeded in making converted Jews 'deny Christ and return to their former error'. This happened, wrote Eadmer, while the king was staying at Rouen. In these cases there may have been another reason, not mentioned by Eadmer, for the king to get involved. In 1096 the religious enthusiasm stirred up by Duke Robert's crusade preparations unleashed a pogrom against the city's substantial and wealthy Jewish community, and many Jews converted to save their lives. In these circumstances Rufus might have thought it right to help those who wished to revert to their previous faith – no doubt in return for a fee. Rufus's father had brought some of Rouen's Jews to London – the first known community in Britain – and may have used them to help finance his conquest of England. According to William of Malmesbury,

> prompted by their gifts and flattery, the king encouraged some Jews of London to debate with Christian bishops, even saying that 'by the holy face of Lucca' if they won, he would become a Jew himself.[18]

Despite the alarms of the clergy the debate was duly held, and the Christians declared the winners, though William of Malmesbury acknowledged that the Jews insisted they had been beaten by partisan passion and not by rational argument. This episode apart, there is nothing to suggest that Rufus had doubts about Christianity. When he thought he was dying in 1093, he seems to have shared the usual anxieties about his soul. In later editions of his history, William of Malmesbury wrote that he supposed the king had been joking when he talked about becoming a Jew. Rufus's jokiness was made to count against him. In his letter to Pope Paschal, Anselm explained that he had not excommunicated Rufus because the king would have acknowledged the sentence only by making fun of it.[19]

Eadmer explicitly noted that he was repeating these tales 'just as they were told to us without asserting or denying their truth or otherwise'.[20] Given that he had his doubts about them, his decision to include them becomes all the more purposeful. Some twentieth-century readers found in them evidence of Rufus as an admirably tolerant and free-thinking individual, but at the time they were intended to explain why Anselm felt he had to resign as archbishop since no reconciliation was possible with a uniquely evil king.

4
Sex in Court

'Into the details of the private life of Rufus it is well not to grope too narrowly.' So wrote Edward Freeman, the Victorian author of the most thorough study of Rufus ever written. Freeman's choice of words implies that he knew the details but preferred not to say. Instead he hinted so broadly that every reader knew what he meant, accusing Rufus of bringing 'the foulest vices of heathendom into a Christian land', and referring to 'the habits of the ancient Greek and modern Turk'.[1] Since then, historians have traded less in innuendo. The finest twentieth-century biographer of the king referred bluntly to 'his homosexuality', and in this century a specialist on same-sex love has claimed that Rufus was 'said by several chroniclers to have been an open sodomite'.[2] At the time the term sodomy referred not specifically to homosexuality but more generally to non-procreative sex, and was thought of as behaviour to which anyone who lacked self-control might sink. But in fact no contemporary or near-contemporary chronicler said that Rufus was a sodomite or that he engaged in sex with men or boys. We do not know whether he was homosexual, heterosexual or bi-sexual. According to Orderic, 'He never took a lawful wife, but gave himself up insatiably to obscene fornications and repeated adulteries.' According to Henry of Huntingdon, Rufus was 'the evil king' who, with his followers, 'indulged unashamedly in unspeakable debauchery'. Exactly what Orderic and Henry meant by those words, or William of Malmesbury meant by 'crimes horrible to mention', is hard to say.[3]

All three of these authors were deeply influenced by Eadmer's narrative. Eadmer too dealt in innuendo, writing in his *Life of Anselm* – which the archbishop himself had read and corrected – that 'almost everyone in the whole kingdom daily gossiped about him [Rufus], saying things in no way befitting royal dignity'.[4] But he did not say what those things were. Anselm himself was notably severe in his condemnation of sodomy and of behaviour such as long hair and effeminate clothes which he believed might encourage it. In the *Historia Novorum*, Eadmer represents Anselm pressing on Rufus the desirability of having a Church council called to check abuses, and telling the king that he was particularly worried about the recent spread of sodomy. A few lines earlier he had accused the fashionable young men of Rufus's court of growing their hair long like girls and walking about with roving eyes, irreligious gestures and mincing steps.[5] In this way he reinforced the connection in the minds of readers between effeminacy and sodomy. By the time Orderic wrote, a generation later, the vision of a debauched and immoral court had taken flight:

During that time effeminate individuals were in positions of influence all over the world and led their dissolute lives in an unbridled way; doomed to burn in the flames of hell, disgusting catamites abandoned themselves entirely and in the foulest manner to the filthy practices of sodomy. They rejected the social conventions of admirable men, scorned the exhortations of priests, and in dress and behaviour persisted in their uncivilised way of life. They parted their hair from the crowns of their heads right down to their foreheads, and grew long and flowing locks just like women; they spent their time eating, and took great pleasure in dressing up in long, tight-fitting shirts and tunics ... At nights they whiled away their time feasting and drinking, in frivolous conversation, playing dice and gambling, and indulging in other ridiculous pastimes, and during the day they spent the whole time sleeping.

Carried away by the intensity of his feeling, Orderic, writing in the 1130s, drifted into the present tense:

Our lascivious youth now embraces the soft ways of the female, and courtiers using every wanton method pay flattering reverence to women. To the toes on their feet they add what look like snakes' tails ... and they sweep the dusty ground with the over-long trains of their robes and cloaks; their hands, whatever they have to do with them, are covered by long and flapping sleeves. So impeded are they by these unnecessary appendages that they are hardly able to walk quickly or indeed do any sort of useful work. They go around with the side parts of their heads shaved, just like thieves, but at the back they let their hair grow long like whores ... These days almost all of our compatriots have taken leave of their senses and now sport natty little beards, publicly proclaiming by such visible evidence that they take delight in sordid pleasures just like stinking billy-goats.[6]

Churchmen who disapproved of long hair in men liked to suggest that flowing locks made them effeminate. In his biography of the English monk-bishop Wulfstan, William of Malmesbury had the bishop 'prophesy' that pre-Conquest Englishmen who wore their hair long would be no better than women when it came to defending their country in the crisis of 1066. This approach occasionally succeeded in getting laymen to cut their hair short, but only temporarily. Whatever monks said, fashionable young men adopted long hair as a marker of their aristocratic status and courtly aspirations. In the 1130s William of Malmesbury noted that some even added hair-extensions. After Rufus's death his successor ostentatiously cleaned up the court, 'restoring the night-time use of lamps and driving out the effeminates'.[7] Henry's propaganda provided fertile soil for nasty stories to flourish. Hugh of Flavigny, in England again in 1100, heard tell of Peter, a royal chaplain, who was actually made pregnant, and whose brother made sacrifices to the devil.[8]

It would be astonishing if the royal household had not seen a good deal of male same-sex activity. It was, like all aristocratic households, overwhelmingly masculine. Stewards, chamberlains, constables, marshals, clerks of the writing office were all male. Then there were the men who looked after the royal hunt, keepers of the hounds, horn-blowers and archers. Apart from laundresses and dairymaids, even the domestic servants were male: cooks, bakers, coopers, butlers, larderers, grooms, carters, sumpter men. As for the courtiers at the political heart of the household, few of them were there full-time. Much of the year they lived on their own estates with their own servants, and if married, with their wives and families. At court, by contrast, they were deprived of their wives and of most of their followers. Here the owners of huge estates and great mansions were compelled to share bed-chambers, even beds, with other men. This was a practice which of itself had no sexual connotation. It was simply taken for granted, and mentioned only when some special circumstance made it newsworthy, as when two former enemies shared a bed as a public statement of reconciliation.

Some provision was made for the sexual urges of the members of the household. In the great crowd that followed the court and the wagons of the household as they incessantly criss-crossed the king's dominions, there were 'troops of effeminates' as well as 'hordes of whores'.[9] One royal servant, tasked with guarding the door to the king's hall, was also required to supervise the prostitutes who followed the court, operating what was in effect a licensed brothel. It could be said of most kings, as Orderic said of Rufus, that his companions were 'soldiers, lechers and common whores'.[10] In royal courts a great deal of what went on met with the disapproval of serious-minded churchmen. Gaimar offered to compose a poem on court life under Henry I, 'the love affairs and the courting, the drinking and the hunting, the festivities and the pomp and ceremony, the acts of generosity and the displays of wealth'.[11] One twelfth-century royal servant, Roland le Pettour, had the duty of performing a leap, a whistle and a fart in the king's presence every Christmas Day.

It may be that Rufus was perceived as protecting sodomites. But for Rufus to thwart Anselm by seeing no need to ban sodomy is one thing; for him to be an active homosexual himself quite another. His personal life remains a closed book. The author of the *Anglo-Saxon Chronicle*, writing after Rufus's death, was deeply critical of the king's violence, avarice and oppression of the Church, but said nothing about his sex life. Hugh of Flavigny, writing before Eadmer published his account, described Rufus as 'a worldly man without fear of God, given to pride and the pleasures of the flesh, hostile to and contemptuous of God's teaching. Yet he would have been a good enough king had he not put a higher value on the kingdom's business than on God's.'[12] In these words there is no hint that Rufus's carnal desires were worthy of special remark. Moreover in Hugh's list of subjects which the papal legate had wished to raise with the king, the only matter of sexual conduct was clerical celibacy, not the king's own sexual behaviour or sodomy. Another well-informed contemporary, also uninfluenced by Eadmer, the Welsh author of the *Chronicle of Princes* (*Brut Y Tywysogyon*), criticized Rufus for iniquity, oppression and injustice. His view was that throughout his life William 'the Red' (Gwilim Goch) had used concubines.[13]

There is evidence for the way in which Rufus was remembered in some quarters in the fears of an Abbess of Wilton, as recorded by Herman of Tournai, for one of the girls in her care:

I was informed that King William had come to look at her. He and his knights had already dismounted and the gates had been opened to them. I was terrified. He was a young king and untamed, who liked to act on impulse, and I feared that when he saw her beauty, he might assault her sexually. I explained the situation to her, and she allowed me to place a veil on her head. The king entered our cloister garden as if to inspect the roses and flowering herbs, but when he saw her with our other girls wearing a veil, he left, showing that he had come only to see her.[14]

Had Rufus been a notorious homosexual, this description of a royal foray into a rose garden would have been an elaborate literary joke, not the sort of practice an author as austere as Herman of Tournai would have indulged in. Another later tale has been interpreted as evidence that Rufus was reputedly homosexual. In this Wace presents us with a courtly king who in jest claimed to be so offended by the crudity of the names of the rivers Cul (arsehole) and Con (cunt) – said to be situated between Alençon and Le Mans – that he decided to keep his feet dry by taking a detour and riding all the way up both of them.[15] Quite apart from the fact that in Maine there are indeed two streams with the names Cul and Acon, no matter how we interpret these lines in the hope of making them shed allusive light on Rufus's sexual behaviour, all that this anecdote unambiguously shows is that he was remembered as a king who was amused by bawdy.

Returning to the strictly contemporary evidence of Anselm's letters, we find that he criticized the king for oppressive treatment of churches, but not for his lifestyle. It cannot be argued that this tells us nothing on the grounds that ecclesiastics customarily refrained from criticizing the sexual morality of kings. Two of Rufus's contemporaries, the Kings of France and Germany, endured fierce criticism on this score, and both were excommunicated – which Rufus never was.

Philip of France was accused, in Orderic's words, 'of rotting away shamefully in the filth of adultery' and in 1095 this led to his excommunication by Urban II. In that same year the German King Henry IV was accused of forcing his queen to submit to sex with his soldiers – an accusation extraordinarily made in public assembly and by the queen herself.

The accusations of sodomy and homosexuality at Rufus's court were vague and unspecific. When named individuals were criticized for sexual excess it was for heterosexual conduct. Ranulf Flambard, for instance, was a well-known philanderer, accused of trying to seduce the daughter of one of his mistresses. As Bishop of Durham he enjoyed teasing the monks of his cathedral chapter by forcing them to dine in his hall where they were served drinks by 'very pretty girls, slim and good-looking, dressed in skin-tight clothes'.[16]

The earl most closely associated with the court was Hugh of Chester, in Orderic's words

> a lover of games and luxuries, actors, horses and hounds and other vanities of this sort. He was always surrounded by a huge household, full of the noise of swarms of boys of both high and humble birth.

Here Orderic was reflecting the overwhelmingly male character of aristocratic households, not hinting that Earl Hugh was a pederast. In any case, he also described Hugh as

> a slave to gluttony who staggered under a mountain of fat, scarcely able to move. Given over to carnal lusts, he had a large progeny of sons and daughters by his concubines.[17]

It is a measure of the gulf that separated monastic and secular values that Hugh, Orderic's bête noire among Rufus's earls, was precisely the one most highly praised by Gaimar for his hospitality and generosity.

Kings and their sons were inevitably offered temptations in many shapes and sizes, and few did not succumb. One twelfth-century chronicler wrote that for a young king to be celibate was a greater miracle than restoring the dead to life. The king's body, particularly when magnificently dressed, was an instrument of politics. Few can have used their body as effectively as Rufus's younger brother did. Henry acknowledged twenty-two bastards by at least fifteen different mistresses. In William of Malmesbury's – ironic? – words, 'All his life he was completely free from fleshly lust, indulging in the embraces of women (as I have heard from those who know) only out of love for fathering children, not to gratify his passions.'[18]

So far as is known – which is not far at all – Rufus had no children. Certainly he never married. But kings' sons, unless pushed into marriage at a young age by their fathers, commonly delayed it until facing a political crisis in which a wife could be useful. The first of the sons of the Conqueror to marry was Robert. He did so in 1100 when he was in his late forties and on his way back from crusade, and needed to raise a huge sum of money in order to recover Normandy peacefully by repaying Rufus what he had lent him. Together with his bride he received from her father, the lord of Brindisi, 'a great quantity of gold, silver and valuables'.[19] Without this (indeed even with it), he might have found recovering Normandy beyond his material and political resources. Henry also married in 1100, on 11 November, three months after he had taken the throne. He married Edith, sister of the King of Scots. This was an alliance intended to shore up his hold on the north, and perhaps also – since on her mother's side she was of royal English descent – as an olive branch to his English subjects at a time when he knew that Robert, having fought his way into Jerusalem, was on his way back to claim the kingdom.

There was a question mark against the validity of Henry's marriage since, as a nun, Edith would have been a 'bride of Christ'. But in 1100 he was desperate, and he managed to persuade Anselm (to the disapproval of many) to give his blessing to the union on the grounds that she had never really been a nun, only spent some years disguised as one for safety's sake. The fact that Eadmer devoted a long section to justifying Anselm's decision shows how defensive he felt about it. Rufus might have been thinking of Edith as a possible wife when he inspected her at Wilton Abbey, but in 1093 there had been no pressing need for him to embark on a questionable marriage. Only in 1088 had he been in such a crisis, and conscious though he was of the need to please English opinion, Edith (born c.1080) and her sisters were then too young for him to marry. If he did have designs on the throne of France, as the historian Suger of Saint-Denis claimed, then he might have considered marrying Philip's daughter. We shall never know.

None of this is to say that Rufus was not homosexual. But if he were, there is no evidence for it. Too many historians – though not all, it should be said – have simply inherited a lurid tradition and embellished it.

1. The Norman kings as imagined by the artist-monk Matthew Paris of St Albans. Three – William I, Henry I and Stephen – hold churches. Only Rufus (top right), holding Westminster Hall, is represented as a secular-minded ruler.

2. Accompanying the text of one of William II's writs in favour of Abingdon Abbey, a king infamous for his taste in footwear (see p. 81) is shown here bearing the sword of justice.

3. Here Bishop Odo is represented as he liked to be seen, as the Conqueror's right-hand man, with his brother Robert of Mortain, a fellow rebel in 1088, on the left. In all probability Odo commissioned the embroidery known as the Bayeux Tapestry and Rufus might well have seen it there.

4. The king's seal. On one side the king enthroned in majesty, on the other the image of a warrior on horseback. The legend on both sides is *Willelmus Dei Gratia* (abbreviated as *Di Gra*) *Rex Anglorum*.

5. An ornamented initial from a twelfth-century manuscript of Anselm of Canterbury's Prayers and Meditations depicting the author as archbishop.

6. A fifteenth-century image of Pope Urban preaching the sermon which launched the First Crusade. Although Rufus, like all the kings of Christian Europe, chose not to join the great march to Jerusalem, it opened the way for him to take Normandy.

7. A penny minted by one of the moneyers licensed by William II. At a time when the penny was a high-value coin, for many the equivalent of a day's wage, Rufus maintained a stable coinage with a high silver content (93–94 per cent fine) and a standardized weight throughout his kingdom.

8. Whereas most kings of England used oaths such as 'By God's teeth' or 'By God's eyes', Rufus preferred – God only knows why – 'By the face of Lucca' (see p. 86). The Holy Face (*Volto Santo*) was a life-size crucifix (from which this is a detail) in Lucca Cathedral.

9. Rufus's reputation as an irreligious man and a formidable enemy to the kings of France is reflected in this fifteenth-century French image of his soldiers setting fire to an abbey.

10. Rochester's strategic importance is highlighted by this magnificent keep, raised in the early twelfth century to complete the stone castle which Rufus had built to replace the wooden one destroyed by his forces during the siege of 1088.

11. A reconstruction of Rufus's Westminster Hall, dominating, as it no longer does, the other buildings of the Palace of Westminster. Westminster Abbey is in the background.

12. Durham Cathedral, like Westminster Hall, was one of the great buildings of Western Europe in the eleventh and twelfth centuries. Raised between 1093 and 1133, it was the architectural achievement of two bishops who served William II, William of St Calais and Ranulf Flambard.

13. A king who ignored God's admonitions to mend his wicked ways receives his come-uppance on 2 August 1100. A fourteenth-century French representation of the most famous moment of Rufus's life.

14. William II was buried in Winchester Cathedral on 3 August 1100. In 1107 the cathedral tower collapsed. As William of Malmesbury observed, it might have done even if the king's body had not been there.

5
Normandy, Maine and Britain

Winning the war of 1088 did not mean that Rufus's brother was no longer dangerous. Odo of Bayeux – that 'fire-breathing dragon', as Orderic called him[1] – was once again at Robert's side. Also at Robert's court was Edgar Atheling, the last surviving male of the English royal dynasty, passed over in 1066 as too young to rule in turbulent times, but a potential threat of uncertain proportions to any Norman king of England. Rufus had cause to be nervous, but so too did Robert. When their brother Henry sailed back to Normandy after being rebuffed by Rufus (see p. 30), he travelled in the company of Robert of Bellême, lord of Alençon and Domfront, key strongholds on Normandy's southern frontier with Maine. Robert suspected both of conspiring with Rufus against him, and arrested them when they landed. William of Malmesbury believed that the duke was too ready to listen to malicious gossip, but he was certainly right to be on his guard. They were eventually released, but not before Earl Roger had also returned to Normandy and put his castles in a state of war-readiness. The underlying political situation was just as unstable as before.

But in February 1091 Rufus met Robert in Rouen and struck a deal. Robert assigned him lordship over

Saint-Valéry-sur-Somme, Cherbourg, Fécamp, the counties of Eu and Aumale, and the castles belonging to Gerard de Gournay and Ralph of Conches. Rufus had achieved a decisive shift in the balance of power, and by what William of Malmesbury called 'his usual methods'.[2] According to the *Anglo-Saxon Chronicle* for 1090,

> by astuteness or by money he got hold of the castle at Saint-Valéry and the harbour, and in the same way he got Aumale and placed knights from his household in it, and they caused damage to the land around by ravaging and burning.

In fact, although unrecorded by any chronicler, Rufus hadn't waited until 1090 before employing his money to win over Norman lords (such as Stephen Count of Aumale) and gain access to their castles and harbours. Robert's charters show that even before September 1089 he had been struggling to keep control of Eu (with its port of Le Tréport) and Gournay. In return for help from his old friend King Philip, he had even given him Gisors, a strategic key to the Vexin. But with the wealth of England against him, it was a losing battle.

No duke of Normandy could ever keep all his barons happy; they quarrelled with each other, usually over disputed inheritance, far too much for that, and those whom the duke disappointed could always turn for help to a king of England, especially one with a reputation for spending freely. Ralph of Conches, for example, egged on in his feud against Count William of Évreux by his wife, Isabel, 'generous, witty and daring who rode to war in armour like a

60

man', accepted a detachment of Rufus's military household and swore allegiance to him.[3] Nor could Robert always rely on King Philip, despite the fact that it was in the latter's long-term interest to prevent England and Normandy falling into the hands of one man. In 1090 Philip mustered a large army to help Robert. In William of Malmesbury's words,

> The king of France, though lazy and surfeited with daily gluttony, came belching and hiccupping to the war, but the money of the king of England met him on the way, with which his resolution melted, he unbuckled his sword-belt and returned to his banqueting.[4]

Not everything went Rufus's way. Among those whose allegiance he bought was a citizen of Rouen named Conan Pilatus, the leader of a faction within the city agitating against the duke. The plan was that while Robert slept soundly in Rouen Castle, Reginald de Warenne and a contingent of Rufus's household troops would ride through the night to find one of the city gates opened to them by Conan's followers. The plot was leaked to Robert just in time for him to ask Henry for help and send urgent summons to William of Évreux and Gilbert de Laigle. On 3 November 1090, as Reginald de Warenne entered by one gate, Gilbert's force crossed the Seine bridge and captured the south gate. Robert and Henry burst out of the castle, but with the whole city convulsed by fierce hand-to-hand street fighting Robert was persuaded to seek safety, leaving Henry in command. In the end those loyal to Robert won the battle.

Reginald de Warenne withdrew, leaving the field clear for a slaughter of Conan's followers. Conan was taken prisoner and brought into the castle. Henry took him to the top of the great tower and invited him to admire the view before pushing him out of a window. 'Conan's Jump' passed into Norman folklore. Nothing else Henry did before becoming king in 1100 made such a big impression.

Up to this point Rufus had still not entered the fray himself, being content to pull strings from a distance. But in February 1091 he crossed the Channel with a large fleet.

> Almost all the Norman magnates eagerly flocked to meet him, bringing him gifts in the hope of receiving greater ones in return. Men from neighbouring provinces, Flanders, Brittany and France, hearing that he was staying at Eu, flocked there too, to experience his munificence and then go home declaring him to be greater than all other princes in wealth and generosity.[5]

Against this display of power Robert could do little but give Rufus what he wanted: formal recognition of his lordship over those parts of Normandy which in practice he already controlled, plus the ports of Cherbourg and Fécamp. In return Rufus promised to restore their lands in England to those who had lost them as punishment for their part in the 1088 revolt. The two brothers promised to help each other recover and retain their paternal inheritance, and declared that if either of them died without a legitimate son, then the other would succeed to the whole. Since neither was married, this was a fraternal declaration to be taken seriously.

And doubtless was taken very seriously by the brother left out. After Henry's signal service to Robert in November 1090, he had good reason to feel aggrieved. He reacted by putting his strongholds at Avranches and Coutances into a state of defence and seizing Mont Saint-Michel. Hence Robert and Rufus's first joint enterprise was to dispossess their brother. As they advanced westwards, nearly all Henry's friends deserted him because, in Orderic's words, 'they feared William's great resources and terrifying power'. At Mont Saint-Michel Henry was helpless against a land and sea blockade. When he ran out of water, he asked for safe conduct and was allowed to go into exile in France.

What Robert wanted from Rufus was help in restoring his authority over Maine, where Helias of La Flèche had been able to establish himself as count. But any such plan was put on hold when news came of a Scottish raid on the north of England in May 1091. The two brothers crossed the Channel and co-operated on a campaign against King Malcolm (see pp. 66–7). Robert stayed on in England for several months after that, but sailed back to Normandy two days before Christmas. The timing of his departure and the fact that Edgar Atheling, whom in February he had been forced to send away, was once again in his company, signal the end of fraternal collaboration. British business meant Rufus had no time for Maine.

Two years later Robert's envoys appeared at Rufus's Christmas court and announced that, unless he went to Normandy and there either kept his promise or gave a satisfactory explanation of why he could not, he would be branded as forsworn. This public threat to his honour had the desired effect. He went to Normandy in early 1094 and met Robert twice. The guarantors to the treaty of 1091 evidently thought Rufus was in the wrong, but he would not accept this. The tension between the brothers, put on hold in 1091, now escalated into war. This time, however, they were more evenly matched, largely because King Philip was no longer quite so easy to bribe; 1094 ended with Duke Robert having had rather the better of the war in Normandy. Consequently Rufus decided that it was time for reconciliation with Henry. He called him to his side and in 1095 sent him 'overseas to Normandy in his service with great treasure. He fought frequently against Robert and did him great damage in both land and men.'[6]

Then a sermon preached in November 1095 changed everything. At Clermont Pope Urban called on men to undertake an armed pilgrimage to Jerusalem. Early in 1096 Duke Robert took the cross, joining the thousands caught up in this unprecedented call to arms. Now he needed money badly, as did all crusaders, and only Rufus had the resources to be able to supply it on the scale required. In return for 10,000 marks Robert mortgaged Normandy to the King of England. How the conflict between the brothers might have gone without this arrangement is impossible to say. In the event Rufus himself took the huge sum (three tonnes of sterling silver) to Rouen in September 1096, and Robert set off on his long march to Jerusalem, accompanied by Odo of Bayeux for whom there was no future in Normandy under Rufus.

Another would-be crusader was Helias Count of Maine.

According to Orderic he came to Rouen and spoke to Rufus:

> 'My lord king, on the pope's advice I have taken the cross of the Lord and vowed to undertake the journey to Jerusalem. As your faithful liegeman I ask for your friendship, hoping to begin my pilgrimage with your guarantee of peace.' The king replied: 'Go wherever you like, but I intend to have the whole of what my father held. Hand Le Mans and the county over to me.'[7]

When Helias said that in that case he would stay and fight under Christ's banner to save his county, Rufus advised him to get his castles ready. In the event Rufus left Robert of Bellême to harass Helias and continued to give higher priority to wars in Britain. He did not return to Normandy until late in 1097 and even then his first concern – as his father's had been – was with the Vexin. Not until Helias had been captured and handed over to Rufus did he make a serious attempt to conquer Maine. By July 1098 he was in possession of Le Mans and all the castles in Maine that his father had once held, a great success celebrated by a triumphant entry into the city.

Until 1097, whenever Rufus crossed the Channel he had been dragged back by threats from the Scots or the Welsh. In 1091, during his first visit to Normandy, 'King Malcolm came from Scotland into England and ravaged a great part of it'. The *Anglo-Saxon Chronicle* says no more, but something of the reality behind those few words can be sensed from the contemporary description by Richard of Hexham of later Scottish raids.

> By the sword's edge or the spear's point, they slaughtered the sick on their beds, women who were pregnant or in labour, babies in their cradles or at their mothers' breasts, and sometimes they killed the mothers too. They slaughtered worn-out old men, feeble old women, anyone who was disabled ... They killed husbands in front of their wives. Then they carried off their plunder and the women, both widows and maidens; stripped, bound and roped together they drove them off, goading them with spears on the way. Their fate was either to be kept as slaves or sold on to other barbarians in exchange for cattle.[8]

'Even today', wrote the early-twelfth-century Durham chronicler Symeon, 'there is scarcely a Scottish household without its English slave, male and female.'[9]

It is a measure of how seriously Rufus and Robert took the Scottish threat that they returned from Normandy in August 1091. Nearly twenty years earlier, by marching an army as far north as Abernethy in 1072, William I had forced Malcolm to end his support for Edgar Atheling (despite the fact that he had recently taken Edgar's sister Margaret as his second wife) and become his client. There were advantages to Malcolm in an arrangement that recognized him as rightful ruler over Lothian (which had been English territory since the seventh century) as well as over the Scots living north of the Firth of Forth. This did not imply that the Scottish kingdom itself was subordinate to England, but it did mean that he had publicly promised not to invade William's territory, and had provided hostages, including his own first-born son, Duncan, as a guarantee of his good faith. No doubt Malcolm regarded his client status as having ended in 1087 with the Conqueror's death – and knew that, thanks to Margaret's fertility, he now had six sons to spare. The raid of 1091 made alarmingly clear to both Robert and Rufus that they must do all they could to restore the agreement that their father had made. And so did the fact that Edgar Atheling had once again been given refuge at the Scottish court. Now that Robert was William's heir, the possibility of a return to King Alfred's line threatened him too.

In response to this double threat, to the lives of their subjects and to their own right to the English throne, the brothers undertook a joint expedition into Scotland, the army marching by the east-coast road and supported by a fleet of fifty grain ships. Although the fleet was wrecked in a storm, this display of power had the desired effect. Malcolm did not dare risk battle against an army which Anglo-Norman industrial strength meant was much better equipped in arms and armour than his own. In the words of the *Anglo-Saxon Chronicle*:

> King Malcolm came to our king and became his man just as he had been to his father, and affirmed it with an oath; and King William promised to restore him the land and all things he had held under his father.

Next year it became clear that Rufus was looking for a more permanent settlement.

1092. In this year King William with a great army went north to Carlisle, and restored the city and built a castle. He drove out Dolfin who had ruled the land there, then garrisoned the castle. After coming back south he sent many farmers there with their women and livestock to live there and cultivate the land.

It is hard to find an earlier example in English history of a king planning to use colonists to consolidate his hold on newly acquired territory. The fact that the writer of the *Anglo-Saxon Chronicle* remarked on it suggests that it was indeed remarkable.

If the takeover of Cumbria shifted the balance of power in the north, it is possible that Malcolm regarded Dolfin of Cumbria as a client of his own, and reckoned that Rufus, by removing him, had broken his side of the 1091 bargain. At any rate in 1093 Malcolm sent an envoy asking Rufus to fulfil his promises. Rufus summoned the Scottish king to meet him at Gloucester on 24 August, providing him with an escort and sending hostages to Scotland for his better security. But when Malcolm reached Gloucester, Rufus refused to meet him unless Malcolm 'did right'. This the Scot then refused to do unless it were on the border between the two kingdoms. The fact that Rufus had sent hostages indicates that he had been keen to speak with Malcolm, but on what subject he wanted Malcolm to 'do right' is far from clear. Since on this trip to England Malcolm also visited his daughter Edith at Wilton Abbey, and was reportedly angry at finding her veiled like a nun,[10] it seems probable that he had come to England in the expectation of arranging a marriage for her, but was then prevented from doing so. He returned to Scotland in anger. Perhaps by refusing to 'do right' except in a symbolic statement of his independence at a meeting on the border, Malcolm had refused to accept that control over her marriage rested as a matter of right with Rufus, as undoubtedly it did as a matter of fact. Since through her mother Edith belonged to the old ruling dynasty of England, this was a matter of high importance.

Whatever the cause of Malcolm's anger, it proved fatal. He hastily mustered an army and launched another raid, only to be ambushed on 13 November by Robert Mowbray, Earl of Northumbria, and killed together with Edward, his oldest son by Margaret. She did not long survive the shock of the deaths of her husband and son. The Scots chose Donald Ban, Malcolm's brother, as king and drove out all the English associated with the previous regime. In this crisis Rufus began to take a more active part in north British affairs than any previous king of England. He encouraged Malcolm's hostage son, Duncan, to go north with English and French support. Duncan had some initial success, but his dependence on outsiders was resented. He hung onto the throne for a while by promising to expel all Englishmen and Normans, but in 1094 he too was killed in Donald Ban's comeback.

Malcolm and Margaret's second son Edgar then became Rufus's candidate for the Scottish throne. He established himself south of the Forth – Lothian still being thought of as part of England – fairly quickly, but not until 1097 did Rufus provide him with enough troops to overcome fierce resistance and set him up in Scotland proper. From then until 1136 the Anglo-Scottish border remained peaceful as Margaret's sons, one after the other, Edgar, Alexander and David, ruled as English client kings. The Anglicization of Scottish society, begun under her aegis, continued apace. William of Malmesbury described it as 'polishing away the rust of Scottish barbarism'.[11] It may be mostly a function of the fact that, in the absence of any contemporary Scottish narratives, the history of north Britain in this period can be viewed only through English eyes, but Rufus, it appeared, had solved not only the Lothian question but also the Scottish one as well.

To a king of England, Wales was a much more intractable problem than Scotland. The Highlands were far beyond his reach and most of what is now southern Scotland was ruled by a single king. Wales, on the contrary, was dangerously close to prosperous English regions and composed of a fluctuating number of small kingdoms – the most substantial being Gwynedd, Powys, Deheubarth, Morgannwg and Gwent – which themselves varied in size according to the changing fortunes of kings who fought each other in incessant ferocious and predatory rivalry. Succession to these precarious kingships was open to any member of the ruling dynasty, even a distant cousin, who had the skills to win men to his side. Between 1069 and 1081 at least eleven Welsh kings and would-be kings were killed or murdered.

Naturally the Welsh raided their English neighbours whenever opportunity offered. But however much a king of England might wish to, it was far from easy for him to get a grip on so kaleidoscopic a polity. William I installed some of his ablest commanders as lords in the marches of Wales, including Hugh of Avranches as Earl of Chester and Roger Montgomery as Earl of Shrewsbury, encouraging them to build castles from Chester to Chepstow. Hugh's cousin Robert was given Rhuddlan and with it, in Orderic's words, 'the duty of defending England against the savage attacks of barbarians'.[12] During the war of 1088 Robert was caught up in events in south-east England, so Welsh raiders seized the chance to sweep into his lands, 'burning, plundering, killing and taking captives'. Not surprisingly: 'For many years Robert had harried the Welsh mercilessly, invading the lands of previously independent people, pursuing them through forests and marshes and over mountains, slaughtering some like cattle, and subjecting others to unlawful slavery.' Even though employed against people he regarded as barbarians, Robert of Rhuddlan's methods caused Orderic, living in a society where slavery was a thing of the past, some distress. 'It is not right that Christians should so oppress their fellow Christians.' In 1093 Robert was killed. While taking a midday nap on the summit of the Great Orme, he was woken by the sounds of uproar on the shore below and realized that seaborne raiders were loading people and animals onto their ships. Reacting angrily to this attack on his territory – his because he had taken it from the Welsh – he rushed down the steep slope without putting on his body armour and was killed. 'In plain sight of his men they cut off his head and fixed it to the mast of a ship as a sign of victory.' A pursuit was called off when the Welsh threw the head overboard.

If 1093 saw a setback for the Normans in north Wales, in the south it was a disastrous year for the Britons – as the Welsh called themselves. Their most prominent king, Rhys ap Twdr of Deheubarth, who had accepted and profited from the status of being William I's client throughout the 1080s, was killed near Brecon. The Normans exploited the ensuing turbulence to make rapid gains along the coast, taking lands as far as Pembroke, Cardigan and Carmarthen. There is no contemporary evidence that Rufus himself took part in this surge westwards, but three of his four recorded stays in Gloucester occurred in 1093. Next year, however, he crossed the Channel in response to Robert's challenge. In the words of the *Brut Y Tywysogyon* (the *Welsh Chronicle*):

> While William was in Normandy, the Britons threw off the rule of the French; being unable to bear their tyranny any longer, they plundered and slaughtered them. They destroyed their castles in Gwynedd and by the end of the year they had destroyed all the castles in Ceredigion and Dyfed except two, Pembroke and Rhyd-y-Gors, and they carried off the people and cattle of Dyfed, leaving it and Ceredigion a wasteland.[13]

In south Wales Rufus left matters to trusted marcher lords such Robert fitz Haimo, lord of Gloucester and conqueror of Glamorgan, but in 1095, after his return to England, and while still in the throes of dealing with rebellion in Northumbria (see p. 78), he judged that the situation in Gwynedd had deteriorated so much that in October he led an army into Snowdonia:

But the Welsh continually withdrew before him, retreating into the mountains and moorland so that they could not be brought to engage. Then the king turned homewards because he saw he could do no more there that winter.[14]

He had no better fortune in an expedition in 1097. According to the near-contemporary *Life of Gruffudd ap Cynan*, ruler of Gwynedd:

When William Longsword received news of Gruffudd's ferocious bravery and of his wars against the French, he took it very badly and roused the whole strength of the kingdom of England against him. He led various squadrons of cavalry and infantry into Gwynedd with which he planned to destroy the inhabitants so completely as not to leave even a dog to piss against a wall. To deprive the weaker side of the protection of woods and forests, he had them cut down ... When Gruffudd heard of this great preparation for war, he placed ambushes in passes where the roads were narrow; in fear of these the king returned to Chester, on the way losing large numbers of wagons, servants and horses. They were prevented from doing damage because Gruffudd's men were practised in attacking sometimes from the front, sometimes from the rear, sometimes from the right, sometimes from the left. Had Gruffudd sent his men against them as they struggled through forests, the king of England and the French would have seen their last day, but he held his men back, just as David had spared Saul.[15]

For all its hyperbole the *Life* gives a good sense of the difficulties confronting those who ventured into the interior of

Wales. The Welsh could melt away and return and rebuild their homes after the alien heavy armour had left. There were no fortified towns or castles to be captured and then held. Such strong points had first to be created. In essence the *Life* tells the same story as the brief narrative in the *Anglo-Saxon Chronicle* which, significantly, ends with the king 'ordering that castles should be erected along the borders'.

For all his great reputation as a soldier it cannot be said that Rufus had much success in Wales. From now on he confined his own war-making to France, where terrain and climate were gentler and enemies more chivalrous. But in his absence and after his death the pressure on Welsh independence continued, making it ever harder for Welsh rulers to call themselves kings. Indeed John of Worcester, writing a generation later, looked back on 1093 as the year when 'kings ceased to rule in Wales'.[16]

6
Secular Society

It was not only churchmen who disliked the way Rufus ruled. The opening words of the charter issued by Henry I on the day of his coronation (5 August) just three days after Rufus had died make that plain.

> I abolish all the evil practices by which the kingdom of England has been unjustly oppressed, and I set out some of those evil customs here.

Most of them related to the ways Rufus had treated secular landowners, and Henry promised to be different. He promised not to make heirs pay exorbitant sums to obtain possession of their predecessor's estate, not to demand payment when granting tenants permission to arrange marriages for the women of their family, not to force his tenants' widows to marry against their will. This was, in effect, Henry's election manifesto, the promise of good government in anticipation of the challenge from Robert which was bound to come. Rufus too, in 1088, had made promises for a like purpose, though if his promises were ever spelled out in detail in writing, no copy of them survived for long – unlike Henry I's coronation charter, which survived to play its part in the making of Magna Carta. We know little more about Rufus's promises than that he was accused of not keeping them. But we know too that neither did Henry I keep the promises he made in 1100.

What the coronation charter reveals is that William the Conqueror's creation of an entirely new aristocracy in England had led to the king enjoying an extraordinary amount of power over his tenants. The new French lords knew that they possessed great estates in England because they had been given them by the king, not because they had inherited them from ancestors. What the king had given, he could take away. Would-be heirs had to pay him an inheritance tax known as a 'relief'. If under age, they and their fathers' estates were taken into custody, allowing the king to pocket the revenues or, if he preferred, grant them and the marriage of his ward to whomever he chose. If there were no close heirs, then, after provision had been made for the widow whose own remarriage was in the king's gift, he could make a new grant of the estate to a man of his own choice. By, for example, giving the heiress to a great estate to one of his followers he could make him a millionaire over the wedding night. So few documents survive from Rufus's reign that specific evidence for this is hard to find; one example might be the marriage of a Lincolnshire heiress, Lucy of Bolingbroke, to Roger de Roumare.

But at all times there were bound to have been people who felt hard done by. In many cases there was not an obvious heir; every choice the king made disappointed at least one other person. In the nature of things there were never enough estates, wards and widows (as well as offices of profit such as sheriffdoms) to satisfy all who aspired to them. No doubt some children and widows had been given in marriage to partners whom the family felt were unsuit-able. In the eleventh and twelfth centuries there was no firm rule about the level of relief; instead it was negotiated on a case-by-case basis. No doubt there were people who felt they had paid too much. What we can see very clearly, thanks to the coronation charter, is that relief, wardship and marriage constituted major points of tension in the structure of the relationship between king and aristocracy. The power which the lord king had over the inheritances and marriages of the richest people in England gave him an exceptionally strong hand in his dealings with the nobility. But it was a hand which had to be played skilfully, if he were not to alienate too many of those families on whose co-operation he ultimately depended. It was very largely by overplaying this strong hand that King John would bring about his regime's downfall. But there was no downfall of Rufus's regime. On the contrary, he was struck down when at the height of power.

Rufus moreover had had to manage the political conse-quences of the fact that between 1087 and 1096 England and Normandy had different rulers. Robert Malet, for instance, paid for his loyalty to Duke Robert by losing the honour of Eye, his great estate in East Anglia and Essex. Rufus gave it to one of the Montgomery brothers, Count Roger 'the Poitevin' – a name Roger acquired as a result of marrying a great heiress from Poitou, a fact which itself made his allegiance all the more worth cultivating. Robert Malet witnessed Henry's coronation charter and no doubt looked forward to the day when the new king would reverse his predecessor's grant of Eye. How many people there were in 1100 who nursed grievances of this sort, and how prominent they were, we shall never know.

What we do know is that in 1095 a few aristocrats were so dissatisfied with Rufus's rule that they rebelled. Their leaders were Robert Mowbray, Earl of Northumbria, the man responsible for killing King Malcolm, and William Count of Eu. According to Orderic, who didn't like the earl – describing him as 'strong, dark, with a severe and miserable face who spoke little and smiled less' – he had robbed some Norwegian merchants.[1] When they complained to Rufus, he ordered the earl to return the stolen goods, but he took no notice. Rufus compensated the merchants in full for their losses and twice summoned Mowbray to court. Unlike the Bishop of Durham in 1088, however, the earl was not given safe conduct, and he refused to come. Rufus marched into Northumbria, captured Newcastle and Tynemouth, then besieged the earl in his great fortress of Bamburgh. Orderic's version of the siege has the earl gloomily watching the construction of siege-works, principally a counter-castle with the traditional name of 'Bad Neighbour', and shouting out from the battlements the names of some of those in the king's army, calling upon them to keep the oaths they had sworn to him. Some may have trembled with fear at hearing their names called. But none moved to join him. Later, while Rufus himself was in Wales (see p. 72), Mowbray broke out, was hunted down and captured in Tynemouth church, where King Malcolm was buried. When Rufus returned he had the earl taken back to Bamburgh, and there threatened to have his eyes put out unless his wife and steward surrendered the castle, which they duly did.

That in the end so few were willing to risk life and limb in open rebellion shows that Mowbray had miscalculated badly, but just what he had calculated is less clear. Had he thought that in his Northumbrian fastness, territory beyond the reach of Domesday Book, he was unassailable? According to John of Worcester, he planned to kill or depose Rufus and replace him with Stephen of Aumale, son of Count Odo of Holderness. But John offered no explanation for their dislike of Rufus. When Geoffrey of Coutances died, Robert had been permitted to succeed to his uncle's West Country estates. Had he paid a greater relief than he liked? No chronicler alleged that Duke Robert had a hand in the rebellion, but given the continuing war between him and Rufus it would be extraordinary if he had not been involved. Mowbray and William of Eu had both supported Robert in 1088, and on the eve of his revolt Mowbray had strengthened his ties with Normans loyal to their duke by marrying Matilda de Laigle. When Robert went on crusade, two of those suspected of involvement in the conspiracy, Stephen of Aumale and Ernulf of Hesdin, went with him. A letter written by Anselm in 1095 reveals that he had been charged with repelling any invaders who landed in Kent. None did, but Rufus evidently thought they might.

The fact that for some it was their second offence explains the greater severity of their punishment. One aristocrat was hanged, William of Eu's cousin and steward William of Andrieu. William of Eu was accused of treason, fought and lost a judicial duel. He had few friends at court – according to Orderic, Earl Hugh of Chester hated him because he mistreated his wife, Hugh's sister – and he was sentenced to be blinded and castrated. More were imprisoned, notably Roger de Lacy, whose estates went to his younger brother Hugh, and Count Odo, whose lordship of Holderness was given to Arnulf, one of the Montgomery brothers. Robert Mowbray himself died twenty years or so later, still in prison.

The lack of support for Mowbray, even at a time when many landowners were caught in a situation of conflicting allegiances to king and duke, suggests that there is much to be said for Gaimar's portrait of Rufus as a ruler who knew how to manage the great men of the realm, always a king's primary task. Because his power of patronage was so great, the court was inevitably a centre of agitation, rivalry and malicious gossip, described in twelfth-century cliché as a hell on earth. In this political hothouse it was important to find ways of lowering the temperature. Gaimar recalled a king whose ready laugh helped smooth over difficult moments. Giffard 'the Poitevin', annoyed over delays to the dubbing of thirty young men whom he had brought to court, staged a demonstration by having them all turn up with their hair cut unfashionably short. Rufus laughed and got twenty of his men to chop off their hair too – 'whereupon head-shearing swept through the whole court' and the subsequent 'knighting was so splendid that men will talk of it for evermore'.[2]

Ceremonial assemblies were the high points of the political year. Here too Rufus followed his father's practice. He, as William of Malmesbury noted, had celebrated the major festivals of the Christian year, Christmas, Easter and Whitsun with sumptuous and magnificent banquets. All the great men were summoned to them by royal command in order that envoys from other nations might admire the large and brilliant company and the splendid luxury of the feast. Foreign visitors were to carry home vivid reports of a generosity that matched his wealth.[3]

On such occasions the king wore his jewels and crown in state. The ostentation of royal trappings of power was meant to dazzle. 'Behold, I see God!' was one observer's response to the gold and precious stones in which the Conqueror had dressed for dinner. This suited Rufus's style too. He liked expensive clothes. So much so that, putting on shoes one morning, he flew into a rage when, according to William of Malmesbury, he discovered how little they had cost. 'You son of a bitch,' he shouted at his valet, 'since when has a king worn such cheap shoes? Get me some that cost at least twice as much.' The monk mocked the king's taste for bling, which he believed made it easy for his servants to cheat him, but appearances mattered. 'Kings', wrote Henry of Huntingdon, 'are like gods to their subjects. So great is the majesty of this earth's highest that people never weary of looking at them. Crowds of women and children rush to gaze at them, so too do grown men and not only frivolous sorts of men.'[4] It was important to put on a good show.

To provide splendid settings for their displays of majesty, kings had great halls built, and none more so than Rufus. Westminster Hall, the hall in Norwich Castle and the Exchequer Hall in Caen, all still stand today and all three were either probably or indubitably built at his command. That Westminster Hall is his is certain. Recent analysis has demolished the old view that his hall must have been an aisled building on the grounds that no one in the 1090s could have created a roof spanning a width of over twenty metres (sixty-six feet) without intermediate support. But they did. It remained the largest hall ever built in medieval England and at the time was the largest in Europe – 'Not half big enough,' was said to have been Rufus's own assessment of its size. The only part of the Palace of Westminster to survive the great fire of 1834, it remained at the heart of England's government for almost eight hundred years, a hubbub of activity and the seat of the central courts of law until the late nineteenth century.

What ordinary people thought of Rufus we shall never know. Some who lived close to the Scottish and Welsh borders might have respected a soldier-king who could deter raiders. Those farmers whom he sent into Cumbria with their wives and livestock to cultivate the land may have been happy to be given a new start, but it would presumably have depended on the terms of their tenancies. (Usually favourable terms were offered in frontier regions in the hope of attracting future settlers.) His wars and his great buildings were expensive. 'Many a man was oppressed because of the work on London Bridge, on the Tower and on the king's hall at Westminster.'[5] Chroniclers complained of heavy taxes in 1090, 1094, 1096, 1097 and 1098, but they complained more about his father's and his brother's taxation than about his. Whereas William I's last geld, the basic land tax, was levied at six shillings per hide, the heaviest rate in Rufus's reign was four shillings per hide. This was in 1096 when he wanted money fast in order to gain peaceful possession of Normandy. Even Anselm, according to Eadmer, was persuaded that this was a 'reasonable and honourable' cause for taxation; the unusually high rate was approved at an assembly of the barons of the whole country.[6] Nonetheless loud protests came from churches far and wide. Bishops and abbots flocked to court, saying they couldn't possibly pay without doing so much harm to poor farmers that they would abandon their fields. To which the courtiers' only reply was: 'Have you no shrines filled with the bones of the dead and adorned with gold and silver?'[7] Kings and courtiers were rarely concerned with the well-being of the poor as long as they remained politically impotent, but it might be thought that in this case the courtiers were pointing the prelates in the right direction. It did not seem so to monks. William of Malmesbury reckoned that his abbot Godfrey who in 1096 stripped the gold off twelve gospel books, eight crosses and eight shrines, was rightly punished by being immediately struck down by scrofula.[8]

7
At War on Land and Sea

By 1099 Rufus had acquired Normandy and conquered Maine; in Britain he had added Cumbria to the lands of the King of England. He could boast of no military achievement to match his father's conquest of England – but then who could? Yet people imagined what he might have done. He was said to have planned to build a bridge of boats to Ireland and conquer it. According to Suger of Saint-Denis, there were many who talked of his scheme to take over the kingdom of France. Had he lived longer, wrote Gaimar, he would have marched on Rome.[1] Even Orderic, who abhorred his treatment of the English Church, could not withhold his admiration for his leadership in war. 'The king was wholly devoted to soldiers, had a special affection for captains at arms and experienced champions.' Orderic listed them: the king's brother Henry, William of Évreux, Hugh of Chester, Walter Giffard and many others who 'led the English king's forces and, so far as the fortunes of war allowed, performed many acts of conspicuous courage'. Outstanding among them was Robert of Bellême, 'surpassing all others in his loyalty to the king and in his cunning':

If Julius Caesar had tried to wrong the king in any way while he had such men about him, even against Caesar and the legions of Rome he would have dared to test the strength and courage of his men.[2]

This was Orderic's explanation for Norman superiority in war against the French. Suger preferred to attribute it to the greater resources available to a ruler 'wonderfully clever in spending the riches of England on hiring and paying soldiers'. But he too acknowledged that the King of England was 'skilled in the art of war'.[3]

One hitherto unnoticed aspect of this is Rufus's management of naval warfare. It was not just by chance that in 1088 a fleet sent to help the rebels was intercepted and suffered heavy losses; not by chance that the garrisons of the coastal fortresses of Pevensey and Rochester were starved into submission; nor by chance that a fleet of supply ships accompanied the invasion of Scotland in 1093. It was not just the accident of geography that Rufus's first recorded action against Duke Robert in 1090 was to take control of the harbour of Saint-Valéry-sur-Somme, the harbour from which his father's fleet had sailed to England in 1066. Nor just accident that his subsequent acquisitions included Le Tréport (the port from which Robert sailed to invade England in 1101), Fécamp and Cherbourg. Despite Rufus's chivalrous reputation, naval warfare, conducted by men whom contemporary chroniclers often referred to as pirates, was rarely chivalrous. William of Malmesbury reported that when Duke Robert's ships were intercepted by the 'king's men guarding the sea' in 1088, many Normans preferred to jump into the sea rather than be taken alive.[4]

That Rufus valued 'his ships' and, as the potential ruler of an Anglo-Norman realm divided by the sea, was well aware of their importance, comes across very clearly in the report of the Bishop of Durham's trial in 1088. In the negotiations to bring the bishop south to stand trial, Rufus's business managers had promised him that if he were sent into exile, then the king would provide the ships needed to take him and his entourage together with their gold, silver, horses, clothes, arms, hounds and hawks, and guarantee them safe passage until they disembarked in France. During the trial itself Rufus insisted that before he provided the ships, 'the bishop must give me his promise that my brother will not, to my loss and against the will of the sailors, retain the ships which I have provided'. Bishop William protested that the king's agents had said nothing of this when negotiating terms with him, and one of the barons, Reginald Paynel, interjected 'yes, it is as the bishop says, that's the promise your earls made and it should be kept'. 'Be silent,' said the king, 'I will not lose my ships because of anyone's pledge.' When the bishop demurred, the king spoke angrily: 'By the face of Lucca, you will not cross the sea until you make this promise about the ships.' The bishop finally made the required promise, and only then was he allowed to go.[5] In this exchange we see a king acutely aware of ships and sea power.

Turning to land warfare, we find that in one respect Rufus differed from both his father and his brothers. Unlike them he never commanded men in a pitched battle. What then did this accomplished and successful commander do when he led his soldiers to war? In the first place there is no doubt that Suger was right. Rufus waged war with money. He took care to maintain a strong and stable coinage, so that men who took the king's silver penny knew what they were getting. He used his cash to buy allegiances, as in his takeover of eastern Normandy in 1090–91. He did so again in 1098–9 in the Vexin, that frontier zone where French and Norman lords who held lands on both sides of the notional border were awkwardly placed when their masters went to war. 'Many of the French worried by the impossibility of serving two masters' chose to open their castles to Rufus as 'the one who had the keener followers and the greater riches'.[6] But the carrot alone was rarely enough. This is how Orderic summarized one campaign:

> In September 1098 King William assembled a huge army and lodged at Conches before crossing into France on 27 September. He advanced rapidly as far as Pontoise, burning, plundering and taking prisoners, in this way destroying that fair region's wealth. The courageous French could not defend their villages against so large a raiding army, and in the absence of their own king dared not risk battle against so powerful a king, guarded by so many troops. Instead they fortified their castles, fought hard in defence of them, and waited for better days.[7]

As this makes clear, the main victims of this kind of war were the villagers and farmers, those who homes were ransacked and burnt. This was how his father had conquered Maine in the 1060s:

his chosen method of conquest was to sow terror in the land by his frequent and prolonged incursions. He devastated vineyards, fields and estates, he seized strongholds and put garrisons in them. In short he relentlessly inflicted innumerable calamities on the land.[8]

Although Rufus fought his wars without ever replicating anything remotely approaching the brutality of his father's harrying of the north of England in 1070–71, it was well known to everyone that war brought suffering to ordinary people. The strategy was clear. In the words of Vegetius, the late-Roman author whose teachings on war were common knowledge, 'The main and principal point in war is to secure plenty of supplies for oneself and to destroy the enemy by famine. Famine is more terrible than the sword.'[9] Famine for the poor meant the impoverishment of lords. 'When the poor have nothing left and can no longer pay their rents, then their lords too find their wealth diminishing.'[10] The kind of warfare fought by Rufus was intended to persuade lords to change sides by putting them under severe economic pressure. It had the additional attraction of enabling his soldiers to enrich themselves by looting.

Even an invasion in overwhelming force such as Rufus's in September 1098 was not entirely risk-free. The larger the force the bigger its stomach, demanding both a supply train of ox-drawn carts and a great deal of foraging and driving-in of cattle and sheep to provide meat on the hoof. But supply trains were vulnerable to attack and so too were the relatively small groups into which it was necessary to divide armies so that they could forage, ravage, burn and plunder. It was common knowledge that, rather than confronting invaders at the first opportunity, it was often better to delay until after they had split up or were on their way home. In 1090 Ralph of Conches ordered his troops, including a detachment from Rufus's military household, to wait until the raiders were withdrawing encumbered by plunder.[11] Good defensive tactics, no doubt, but the farmers paid the price. In this kind of war clashes between plundering or foraging parties and reconnaissance patrols were frequent. These gave plenty of opportunities for displays of prowess, bravery and cunning.

If territory in France and England was to be won and held, then strongholds had to be taken. In England the war of 1088 turned on the capture of Tonbridge, Pevensey, Rochester; the war of 1095 on the capture of Newcastle, Morpeth and Bamburgh. In the Vexin Rufus's main targets were the fortresses of Pontoise, Mantes and Chaumont. By 1100 he still had not taken them, but Chaumont was under severe pressure as a consequence of his building a new castle at Gisors, recently recovered from the French. Robert of Bellême chose the site and design of a fortress which was to be one of Normandy's greatest frontier castles. It was one thing to build a castle, another to supply it. By sending farmers to Cumbria Rufus was providing his new fortress town at Carlisle with vital economic hinterland.

In siege warfare too the main weapon was hunger. Only rarely was it possible to take a well-fortified place quickly, and close assault was very risky. In 1099 Rufus attacked the castle of Mayet. His men worked to fill the ditch with piles of wood and build a bridge across it, but the defenders hurled down buckets of burning charcoal and set the infilling ablaze.

While Rufus was contemplating this setback, a stone hurled from a tower smashed the head of the man standing next to him, followed by loud laughter and shouts from above – 'Look, now the king has some fresh meat! Take it to the kitchen and serve it up for his dinner!' (presumably a joke at the expense of Rufus's obsession with supplies). His people persuaded him to call the siege off. Next morning they set about laying waste the surrounding region, uprooting vines, cutting down fruit trees and smashing walls and fences.[12]

Twelfth-century commentators all agreed that Rufus's finest military achievement was his capture of one of great cities of medieval France, Le Mans. What Rufus, Helias of La Flèche and Robert of Bellême said and did during the war for Maine became the stuff of legend, causing even Thomas Becket's friend, John of Salisbury, author of a Life of Anselm intended to promote the archbishop's canonization, to include Rufus in a short list of great commanders.[13] Orderic's narrative of the campaign reveals a monk's view of war's central ingredients: money, supplies and rapid exploitation of good information. Rufus's first aggressive move against Helias came in February 1098 at Robert's urging. Annoyed at the way the castle of Dangeul had been disrupting his ravaging of the district, he persuaded Rufus that it could be taken in a surprise winter attack. But Helias learned of their plans and took effective counter-measures, mustering his troops and deploying them at key points such as river crossings and paths through the woods. Disappointed, Rufus returned to Normandy, leaving Helias to take the initiative by raiding Bellême territory. Returning home at the end of one raid, while still separated from the main body of his troops, Helias led a handful of knights in a charge against what he thought was a small contingent, only to be captured when ambushed by Robert's larger force.

Seizing the opportunity, Rufus mustered an exceptionally big army and in June 1098 headed for Le Mans. Local lords, unable to resist but unwilling to be seen as the first to surrender, negotiated truces with a king who appreciated their predicament and allowed them to await the outcome of events in and around Le Mans. With no fighting or ravaging to slow his advance, Rufus soon had the city under siege.

> Outside the walls fine feats of arms were performed on both sides. Renowned champions from the two forces competed to show their valour and earn the laurels of war from their leaders and fellow-soldiers.[14]

But Le Mans was a tough nut to crack. As soon as the news of Helias's capture had come through, the city had opened its gates to Maine's overlord, Count Fulk of Anjou, and he had laid in plenty of supplies. The large besieging army felt the pinch first. The time of year, Orderic noted, meant that not much of the previous harvest remained, while it was still too early for this year's.

Once again Rufus withdrew to Normandy, once again ceding the initiative to his opponents. Fulk laid siege to Ballon, an important castle to the north of Le Mans of which Rufus had made Robert captain. The garrison immediately sent a message to Rufus, but by the time he came to their relief they had already won the war for him. So good was the garrison's information about what was happening in the besiegers' camp that they were able to sally out and catch them at lunch and at ease. Count Fulk escaped but many were captured, including four lords whose support he could ill afford to lose. As a consequence Rufus and Fulk rapidly came to terms. All prisoners were to be released, Helias included, and in return the king was given possession of Le Mans and all the castles which his father had held. It was a great triumph, won, Orderic noted, without much bloodshed.

Rufus strengthened the citadel and installed a garrison, well provided with 'arms, food and every kind of supply'. But next summer, while Rufus was in England, Helias re-entered the city and laid siege to the citadel. The garrison sent an envoy to find Rufus, while the siege turned into a war of attrition and artillery duel. Much of the city and its suburbs were destroyed by a fire started by a flaming missile launched from one of the siege machines in the citadel. The moment Robert of Bellême's envoy Amalchis (so important was his message and so impressive his speed that his name was remembered) brought the news, Rufus was off. 'Point me', he said, 'in the direction of Le Mans and I shall head straight there.'[15] As told by Wace, he demonstrated his resolve not to deviate an inch by tearing down the palace wall that stood in his way. At the coast he embarked in the first ship he could find, despite being advised by the helmsman to wait until the storm had abated.

Silence, brother! You've never before seen a king drown, and I'm certainly not going to be the first![16]

Even Eadmer acknowledged the power of this tale.

On landing at Touques (see above p. 11) the king raced towards Le Mans, collecting more troops en route. Helias and his men had still not been able to take the citadel when they heard that Rufus was approaching fast. 'Terrified by fear of the king' – the words are those of an anonymous Le Mans cleric – they left in a hurry. The citizens, already traumatized by the state of their city and now shocked to be deserted by their count, followed, taking their women and children, but abandoning everything else in the fire-damaged ruins. After a brief pursuit of Helias and the siege of Mayet, Rufus returned to enter Le Mans for a second time. 'Had not the king's liberality checked the rapacity of rampaging plunderers, our city would have been totally destroyed.'[17] But he also caused consternation by ordering the demolition of the towers of the cathedral on the grounds that they had been employed as fire-platforms by Helias. He was, wrote this same anonymous author, who had good reason to know, 'like a fierce lion in the terror he caused to his own and neighbouring people, rich, confident in his courage, glorying in the great number of his forces and in his vast wealth'.[18]

According to Suger, one of the ways Rufus employed his great riches was in immediately paying the ransoms of any of his men who were captured. By contrast he would not release French knights unless they had sworn allegiance to him and promised to fight against the King of France. One of those who swore such an oath was Nivard, lord of Septeuil (south of Mantes). Nivard accompanied Rufus when the king led a raid deep into Capetian territory south of Paris late in 1098, but then had second thoughts. He took his oath to Rufus seriously enough to have Ivo Bishop of Chartres absolve him from it. Rufus sent the bishop a letter of protest. Should not Christians always keep the promises they have made to fellow Christians? Ivo's answer was yes, but Nivard had earlier sworn an oath of allegiance to the King of France, 'his natural and lawful lord'. He had been wrong to make that promise to Rufus, and for that the bishop had imposed a penance.[19] But Rufus was celebrated for believing in, and practising, a knightly code of honour, and it seems likely that he would have regarded these as a lawyer's weasel words.

When the prisoners held in Ballon in 1098 heard the castle garrison's jubilation as Rufus's relieving army arrived, they

> all shouted together at the top of their voices, 'William, noble king, free us'. Hearing the shouts he ordered them to be released at once and given a good meal in the courtyard outside with his own men, releasing them on parole until after dinner. When his followers objected that in such a crowd of people they might easily escape, he said 'I cannot possibly imagine that an honourable knight would break his sworn word. If he did, he would be despised for ever as an outcast.'[20]

This, a very early instance of parole, perhaps the earliest in European history, suggests that Rufus would have looked upon Nivard as an outcast who broke his sworn word. Had Nivard been one of his own subjects, he might well have taken a different view, but in a world of conflicting loyalties Rufus stood out as a ruler unusually devoted to chivalric values. Indeed the war for Le Mans went into a second round in 1099 because Rufus had released Helias, despite the count's proud insistence that he would take up the fight again as soon as he was able. In one version of an exchange between the two men that became legendary, William of Malmesbury emphasized Rufus's admiration for Helias's bold words and his generosity in letting him go in 1098 without trying to recapture him on the way home.

> Sod off then, you clown! Get out! You've my permission to do your worst. And, by the face of Lucca, if you beat me, I shall ask for nothing from you in return for letting you go now.[21]

Rufus, Orderic commented, 'was not cruel in his treatment of knights, but gracious and generous, courteous and good-humoured'.[22]

His reputation for ransoming his men quickly – a practice doubtless intended to persuade them not to switch sides – had the disadvantage, according to Orderic, of encouraging the French to fight hard, spurred on by the hope of becoming rich. It also meant that they fought to capture rather than to kill. They fought vigorously but,

> forgetting neither their fear of God nor their common humanity, they thoughtfully and generously spared the persons of their enemies and turned the force of their anger against their valuable chargers ... The dogs and birds of France gorged themselves on horseflesh.[23]

This was evidently not how Malcolm and Edward of Scotland had been treated by Robert Mowbray in 1093. Orderic thought they had been killed without warning when unarmed. 'At this news the king of England and his magnates were grieved beyond measure that such a disgraceful and cruel deed should have been perpetrated by Normans.'[24] The circumstances may not have been quite as bad as Orderic believed, but many twelfth-century authors felt uneasy about the way Malcolm and Edward died. Besides, a dead king was not as useful a bargaining chip as a captured one.

War on England's northern and western frontiers was not conducted in the same chivalrous spirit as in France. When Archbishop Hugh of Lyons wrote to Rufus in 1099 he addressed him as 'the victorious king of the English', and referred explicitly to his victories over 'barbarous nations', by which he meant the Scots and the Welsh. In Britain Scottish and Welsh raiders still hunted down and carried off women and children old enough to work along with the rest of the desirable livestock. In France, by contrast, where slavery no longer existed, only those people wealthy enough to be ransomed were worth the trouble of capturing; the rest would be killed if they resisted but otherwise allowed to run away. In France wars were fought between men who were often linked by ties of family and who spoke the same language. It was in this French and chivalrous kind of warfare that Rufus was most at home.

8

Assassination

'The victorious king' was killed at the height of his power. In William of Malmesbury's words,

> He formed mighty plans and would have been mightily successful had he lived longer. His energy of mind was such that no kingdom was beyond the reach of his ambition. On the day before he died, when asked where he would celebrate Christmas, he replied 'Poitiers', because it was thought that the duke of Aquitaine wanted to go to Jerusalem and was about to mortgage his land to him for cash.[1]

But about that scheme we have almost no other evidence. In practice historians of Rufus's reign have concentrated on Church-State relations because that is where the bulk of the evidence is – provided by Anselm's letters and Eadmer's two books. To Anselm and Eadmer matters of principle involving God and man were on a vastly higher plane than the mundane and unpleasant business of going to war and raising the money to pay for territorial aggrandizement. At the time very few others shared their priorities. Nonetheless nothing has shaped Rufus's reputation more than his quarrel with Anselm. In that sense, and with hindsight, it can be seen that his appointment of Anselm, the saintly theologian whose 'proof' of the existence of God continues to be discussed today, was Rufus's greatest blunder. Anselm lacked Lanfranc's political nous, but as a teacher he inspired devotion and Rufus was extraordinarily unlucky in that the leader of Anselm's fan club was a biographer whose vivid prose succeeded in bringing back to life both the dead archbishop and the dead king. In defending Anselm's extraordinary decision to leave England, Eadmer set out to destroy Rufus's reputation.

His success can be most plainly seen by comparing what Orderic wrote about Rufus in France, a subject on which Eadmer said nothing, with what he wrote about the king in England. In England Rufus was the oppressor of the Church; in Normandy he was both a popular (see above p. 11) and chivalrous war leader and an admirably strong ruler. According to Orderic, the churches of Normandy even appealed to Rufus to save them from the disorder from which they were suffering under his brother's rule. Admittedly this is chiefly a reflection of Orderic's hostility to Robert, but it is noticeable that he was quite neutral on the subject of Rufus's appointments to Norman Church office.[2] His comment on the impact of Rufus's death on Normandy laments the Red King's passing:

Many who had been nursing anger and hatred but had not dared take vengeance openly because of the strict justice enforced by the ruler, fell upon each other without restraint, now that control had been relaxed.[3]

Historians of English monarchy have naturally paid much more attention to what Orderic wrote about England than to what he wrote about Normandy.

Rufus's reputation was vulnerable in other ways. He was inevitably overshadowed by his father; all Norman landowners and their descendants in Britain had reason to celebrate the Conquest, and much less reason to remember the Conqueror's son. After the civil wars of Stephen's reign Henry II would look back to the reign of his grandfather Henry I as the good old days of good kingship. That model of kingship's most famous document, his coronation charter, began by referring to the oppression endured by the kingdom under his predecessor. Whether or not Rufus intended to marry, he did not. He left few to cultivate his memory – perhaps only the monks of Battle Abbey – and certainly no known descendants.

In all likelihood the fatal arrow was shot by Walter Tirel, lord of Poix in north-east France, but there is simply not enough evidence to decide whether it struck Rufus by accident or design. All advocates of the murder theory see someone else's mind behind Walter's bowshot. Rufus's brother Henry, and the King of France, or his son Louis, are the usual suspects, but many others from the pope downwards have been suggested. According to John of Worcester, the plotters of 1095 had planned to kill or depose Rufus, and perhaps they had. But Henry seems to have lived more in fear of assassination than his brother had. According to Suger, he slept in a different place each night after one of his own staff tried to kill him, and never went to bed without a sword and shield by his side.[4] William of Malmesbury, who knew Henry's court well, reported that the king believed that only his coat of mail had saved him from the arrow of one of his own subjects.[5] One of Henry's own daughters shot at him with a crossbow after he had mutilated her children.[6] We cannot say whether or not Rufus was assassinated; we can be more confident that he was the target of an attempted character assassination.

Notes

1. THE PERSONALITY OF THE KING:
EVIDENCE AND INTERPRETATIONS

1. Eadmer, *Historia Novorum* (*The History of Novelties*), ed. Martin Rule (London: Longman, 1884), p. 224.
2. Eadmer, *Historia*, p. 116; *Eadmer's History of Recent Events in England*, trans. Geoffrey Bosanquet (London: Cresset Press, 1964), p. 121. This translation goes only as far as p. 216 of Martin Rule's edition.
3. Geffrei Gaimar, *Estoire des Engleis* (*History of the English*), ed. and trans. Ian Short (Oxford: Oxford University Press, 2009), p. 321.
4. *Eadmer's History*, p. 27.
5. William of Malmesbury, *Gesta Pontificum Anglorum* (*The History of the English Bishops*), vol. 1: *Text and Translation*, ed. and trans. M. Winterbottom (Oxford: Clarendon Press, 2007), p. 109; *The Deeds of the Bishops of England*, trans. David Preest (Woodbridge: Boydell Press, 2002), p. 50.
6. *Eadmer's History*, p. 51.
7. *Anglo-Saxon Chronicle* (various editions), 1087.
8. *The Ecclesiastical History of Orderic Vitalis*, ed. and trans. Marjorie Chibnall, 6 vols (Oxford: Clarendon Press, 1969–80), vol. 5, pp. 203, 293.
9. Orderic Vitalis, vol. 5, p. 257.
10. William of Malmesbury, *The History of the English Kings* (*Gesta Regum Anglorum*), ed. and trans. R. A. B. Mynors, R. M. Thomson and M. Winterbottom, vol. 1 (Oxford: Clarendon Press, 1998), p. 543.
11. *History of the English Kings*, pp. 551, 567.
12. *History of the English Kings*, pp. 555–7, 567.
13. *History of the English Kings*, pp. 543, 555.
14. *History of the English Kings*, pp. 560–61.
15. Edward A. Freeman, *The Reign of William Rufus and the Accession of Henry the First*, 2 vols (Oxford: Clarendon Press, 1882), vol. 1, p. 157; vol. 2, p. 337.
16. A. L. Poole, *From Domesday Book to Magna Carta 1087–1216*, *The Oxford History of England*, vol. 3 (2nd edn, Oxford: Clarendon Press, 1955), p. 99.

2. TAKING THE THRONE

1. *History of the English Kings*, p. 543.
2. *History of the English Kings*, p. 551.

3. *Asser's Life of King Alfred*, ed. W. H. Stevenson (Oxford: Clarendon Press, 1959), p. 59.
4. *Orderic Vitalis*, vol. 4, p. 121.
5. *History of the English Kings*, p. 493.
6. *History of the English Kings*, p. 711.
7. *Orderic Vitalis*, vol. 2, p. 359.
8. *History of the English Kings*, p. 543.
9. The *Gesta Normannorum Ducum*, vol. 2, ed. and trans. Elisabeth Van Houts (Oxford: Clarendon Press, 1995), p. 187.
10. *Orderic Vitalis*, vol. 4, pp. 101–7.
11. *Eadmer's History*, p. 26.
12. 'Acta Lanfranci', in *English Historical Documents (EHD)*, vol. 2 (1042–1189), ed. D. C. Douglas and G. W. Greenaway (London: Routledge, 1981), p. 679.
13. *Anglo-Saxon Chronicle*, 1088.
14. *Orderic Vitalis*, vol. 4, p. 279.
15. *Orderic Vitalis*, vol. 4, p. 159.
16. *Anglo-Saxon Chronicle*, 1088.
17. *History of the English Kings*, p. 547.
18. *Orderic Vitalis*, vol. 4, p. 135.
19. *EHD*, pp. 658–64.

3. THE ENGLISH CHURCH

1. *The Life of St Anselm by Eadmer*, ed. and trans. R. W. Southern (London: Thomas Nelson & Sons, 1962), p. 63.
2. Symeon of Durham, *Libellus de Exordio atque Procursu istius hoc est Dunhelmensis Ecclesie*, ed. and trans. David Rollason (Oxford: Clarendon Press, 2000), p. 243.
3. *The Chronicle of Battle Abbey*, ed. and trans. Eleanor Searle (Oxford: Clarendon Press, 1980), pp. 97–9.
4. *Anglo-Saxon Chronicle*, 1097.
5. *Eadmer's History*, pp. 96–7; also in Sally N. Vaughn, *Archbishop Anselm 1093–1109* (Farnham: Ashgate, 2012), p. 217.
6. *Eadmer's History*, p. 87.
7. Vaughn, *Archbishop Anselm*, p. 221.
8. Anselm's letters, no. 176, written in 1094, in *Sancti Anselmi Cantuariensis Archiepiscopi Opera Omnia*, ed. F. S. Schmitt (Edinburgh: Thomas Nelson & Sons, 1946–51).
9. William of Malmesbury, *Gesta Pontificum*, pp. 91–3.
10. *Eadmer's History*, p. 85.
11. Henry of Huntingdon, *Historia Anglorum*, ed. and trans. Diana Greenway (Oxford: Clarendon Press, 1996), p. 587.
12. *The Correspondence of Pope Gregory VII*, ed. E. Emerton (New York: Columbia University Press, 1932), p. 169.
13. *Eadmer's History*, pp. 55–62.
14. Hugonis Chronicon, *Monumenta Germaniae Historica*, Scriptores, vol. 8 (Hanover: 1848), p. 475.
15. *Eadmer's History*, p. 86.
16. *Eadmer's History*, p. 106.
17. *Eadmer's History*, pp. 103–5.

18. *History of the English Kings*, p. 563.
19. Vaughn, *Archbishop Anselm*, p. 223.
20. *Eadmer's History*, p. 103.

4. SEX IN COURT

1. Freeman, *Rufus*, vol. 1, pp. 157, 159.
2. Frank Barlow, *William Rufus* (London: Methuen, 1983), p. 436; William Burgwinkle, *Sodomy, Masculinity and Law in Medieval Literature* (Cambridge: Cambridge University Press, 2004), p. 49.
3. *Orderic Vitalis*, vol. 5, p. 203; Henry of Huntingdon, p. 449; William of Malmesbury, *Deeds of the English Bishops*, p. 67.
4. *Life of St Anselm*, p. 64.
5. *Eadmer's History*, pp. 49–50.
6. *Orderic Vitalis*, vol. 4, pp. 186–8.
7. *History of the English Kings*, p. 715.
8. Hugonis Chronicon, pp. 496–7.
9. *History of the English Kings*, p. 561.
10. *Orderic Vitalis*, vol. 5, p. 293.
11. Gaimar, *Estoire*, p. 353.
12. Hugonis Chronicon, p. 495. Compare the similar judgement in the work of another French monk, also uninfluenced by Eadmer, in Hugh of Fleury's *Liber qui modernorum regum Francorum continet actus*, MGH SS 9, p. 392.
13. *Brut Y Tywysogyon, Red Book of Hergest Version*, ed. and trans. Thomas Jones (Cardiff: University of Wales Press, 1955), p. 41.
14. Herman of Tournai, *The Restoration of the Monastery of Saint Martin of Tournai*, trans. Lynn H. Nelson (Washington, DC: Catholic University of America Press, 1996), pp. 31–2.
15. Wace, *The Roman de Rou*, trans. Glyn S. Burgess (St Helier: Société Jersiaise, 2002), pp. 307–9.
16. William of Malmesbury, *Gesta Pontificum*, p. 417.
17. *Orderic Vitalis*, vol. 2, p. 263; vol. 3, p. 217.
18. *History of the English Kings*, p. 745.
19. *Orderic Vitalis*, vol. 5, p. 281.

5. NORMANDY, MAINE AND BRITAIN

1. *Orderic Vitalis*, vol. 4, p. 149.
2. *History of the English Kings*, p. 549.
3. *Orderic Vitalis*, vol. 4, p. 213.
4. *History of the English Kings*, p. 549.
5. *Orderic Vitalis*, vol. 4, p. 236.
6. *Anglo-Saxon Chronicle*, 1095.
7. *Orderic Vitalis*, vol. 5, pp. 229–31.

8. Alan O. Anderson, *Scottish Annals from English Chroniclers* (London: David Nutt, 1908), pp. 180, 187.
9. Anderson, *Scottish Annals*, p. 93.
10. *Eadmer's History*, p. 128.
11. *History of the English Kings*, p. 727.
12. This and the following quotations from *Orderic Vitalis*, vol. 4, pp. 137–43.
13. *Brut Y Tywysogyon*, p. 35.
14. *Anglo-Saxon Chronicle*, 1095.
15. *Vita Griffini filii Conani*, ed. and trans. Paul Russell (Cardiff: University of Wales Press, 2005), p. 79.
16. *The Chronicle of John of Worcester*, vol. 3, ed. and trans. P. McGurk (Oxford: Clarendon Press, 1998), p. 65.

6. SECULAR SOCIETY

1. *Orderic Vitalis*, vol. 4, p. 279.
2. Gaimar, *Estoire*, pp. 329–31.
3. *History of the English Kings*, p. 509.
4. *History of the English Kings*, pp. 557–8; Henry of Huntingdon, *Historia*, p. 605.
5. *Anglo-Saxon Chronicle*, 1097.
6. *Eadmer's History*, p. 78.
7. *History of the English Kings*, p. 563.
8. William of Malmesbury, *Deeds of the English Bishops*, p. 297.

7. AT WAR ON LAND AND SEA

1. Gaimar, *Estoire*, pp. 323–5.
2. *Orderic Vitalis*, vol. 5, p. 215.
3. Suger, *Vie de Louis VI le Gros*, ed. and trans. Henri Waquet (Paris: Librairie ancienne Honoré Champion, 1929), pp. 7–9.
4. *History of the English Kings*, p. 549.
5. *EHD*, pp. 657, 663–5.
6. *Orderic Vitalis*, vol. 5, p. 215.
7. *Orderic Vitalis*, vol. 5, pp. 217–19.
8. The *Gesta Guillelmi* of William of Poitiers, ed. and trans. R. H. C. Davis and Marjorie Chibnall (Oxford: Clarendon Press, 1998), p. 61.
9. Vegetius, *Epitome of Military Science*, trans. N. P. Milner (Liverpool: Liverpool University Press, 1993), p. 65.
10. *History of William Marshal*, ed. A. J. Holden, trans. S. Gregory, vol. 1 (London: Anglo-Norman Text Society, 2002), p. 35.
11. *Orderic Vitalis*, vol. 4, p. 216.
12. *Orderic Vitalis*, vol. 5, pp. 259–61.
13. John of Salisbury, *Policraticus,* trans. J. Dickinson (New York: Russell & Russell, 1963), book 6, chapter 18.

14. *Orderic Vitalis*, vol. 5, p. 243.
15. Wace, *Roman de Rou*, p. 307.
16. Gaimar, *Estoire*, p. 317.
17. *Actus Pontificum Cenomannis in urbe degentium*, ed. G. Busson and A. Ledru (Le Mans: Archives historiques du Maine, 1901), p. 402.
18. *Actus Pontificum Cenomannis*, p. 404.
19. Ivo of Chartres, in *Patrologia Latina*, ed. J. P. Migne (221 vols, Paris: 1844–64), vol. 162, letter no. 71.
20. *Orderic Vitalis*, vol. 5, p. 245.
21. *History of the English Kings*, p. 567.
22. *Orderic Vitalis*, vol. 5, p. 239.
23. *Orderic Vitalis*, vol. 5, p. 219.
24. *Orderic Vitalis*, vol. 4, p. 271.

8. ASSASSINATION

1. *History of the English Kings*, p. 577.
2. *Orderic Vitalis*, vol. 4, pp. 179–81; vol. 5, pp. 211–13.
3. *Orderic Vitalis*, vol. 5, p. 301.
4. Suger, *Vie de Louis*, p. 190.
5. *History of the English Kings*, pp. 727–9.
6. *Orderic Vitalis*, vol. 6, pp. 213–15.

Further Reading

First published in 1983, Frank Barlow, *William Rufus* (reprint, New Haven and London: Yale University Press, 2000) remains the standard full-length life, remarkable for its portrayal of aristocratic society as well as of the reign. Emma Mason, *William II: Rufus, the Red King* (Stroud: Tempus, 2005), even if it does not, as the publisher claimed, 'reveal for the first time the truth behind the king's death', nonetheless offers a serious analysis of his life.

William M. Aird, *Robert Curthose, Duke of Normandy c.1050–1134* (Woodbridge: Boydell, 2008) and Judith A. Green, *Henry I King of England and Duke of Normandy* (Cambridge: Cambridge University Press, 2006) are the two best studies of Rufus's brothers. The most recent biography of his father is David Bates, *William the Conqueror* (New Haven: Yale University Press, 2016). Less daunting is Mark Hagger, *William: King and Conqueror* (London: I. B. Tauris, 2012).

The chapter on Rufus in David Crouch, *The Normans: The History of a Dynasty* (London: Hambledon, 2002), is characteristically lively and misguided. Christopher Brooke, *The Saxon and Norman Kings* (London: Batsford, 1963) provides a usefully long perspective and on Rufus sensible scepticism.

On Anselm and Eadmer the work of R. W. Southern is fundamental, notably *Saint Anselm: A Portrait in a Landscape* (Cambridge: CUP, 1990), a rethinking of his earlier *St Anselm and his Biographer* (Cambridge: CUP, 1963). Some key letters are helpfully provided in both Latin and English translation by Sally N. Vaughn, *Archbishop Anselm 1093–1109: Bec Missionary, Canterbury Primate, Patriarch of Another World* (Farnham: Ashgate, 2012); she rightly sees Rufus as a 'much-maligned king'. On the historians of the next generation the basic studies are Marjorie Chibnall, *The World of Orderic Vitalis* (Oxford: Clarendon Press, 1984); Rodney M. Thomson, *William of Malmesbury* (2nd edn, Woodbridge: Boydell, 2003); John Gillingham, 'The Ironies of History: William of Malmesbury's Views of William II and Henry I', in Rodney M. Thomson, E. Dolmans and E. Winkler (eds), *Discovering William of Malmesbury* (Woodbridge: Boydell, 2017); 'Kingship, Chivalry and Love. Political and Cultural Values in the Earliest History Written in French: Geoffrey Gaimar's *Estoire des Engleis*', in John Gillingham, *The English in the Twelfth Century* (Woodbridge: Boydell, 2000).

Those already familiar with an outline of events will find in the first five chapters of Robert Bartlett, *England under the Norman and Angevin Kings 1075–1225* (Oxford: OUP, 2000) a brilliant analysis of political structures over a longer timespan. Two key articles on the politics of the reign are C. P. Lewis, 'The King and Eye: A Study in Anglo-Norman Politics', in *English Historical Review*, 104 (1989), pp. 569–89 and Richard Sharpe, '1088 – William II and the Rebels', in *Anglo-Norman Studies*, 26 (2003–4); also two essays, 'The Strange Death of William Rufus' and 'Magnates and "Curiales" in Early Norman England', in C. Warren Hollister, *Monarchy, Magnates and Institutions in the Anglo-Norman World* (London: Hambledon Press, 1986). See also Judith A. Green, *The Aristocracy of Norman England* (Cambridge: CUP, 1997). For the latest thinking on Domesday Book and on Ranulf Flambard's career see Sally Harvey, *Domesday Book of Judgement* (Oxford: OUP, 2014).

Two important books on the conduct of war are J. O. Prestwich, *The Place of War in English History 1066–1214*, ed. Michael Prestwich (Woodbridge: Boydell, 2004) and Matthew Strickland, *War and Chivalry: The Conduct and Perception of War in England and Normandy, 1066–1217* (Cambridge: CUP, 1996).

The best introduction to courtly attitudes to sex, though inevitably – given the absence of relevant eleventh-century sources – on a rather later period is John W. Baldwin, *The Language of Sex: Five Voices from Northern France around 1200* (Chicago and London: University of Chicago Press, 1994). Homoerotic feelings are given their due in William Burgwinkle, *Sodomy, Masculinity and Law in Medieval Literature: France and England, 1050–1230* (Cambridge: CUP, 2004).

For the most recent scholarship on the buildings associated with Rufus see Edward Impey and John McNeill, 'The Great Hall of the Dukes of Normandy at Caen', in J. A. Davies, J.-M. Levesque and A. Riley (eds), *Castles and the Anglo-Norman World. Proceedings of a Conference held at Norwich Castle Museum in 2012* (Norwich: 2015); and R. B. Harris and D. Miles, 'Romanesque Westminster Hall and its Roof', and Edward Impey, 'The Great Hall at Caen and its Affinities with Westminster', both in W. Rodwell and T. Tatton-Brown (eds), *Westminster: The Art, Architecture and Archaeology of a Royal Abbey and Palace* (British Archaeological Association Conference Transactions for 2013, vol. 39, forthcoming).

Picture Credits

1. Portraits of four kings of England: William the Conqueror and William II (above); Henry I and Stephen (below), illustration from *Historia Anglorum*, 1250–59 (© The British Library Board [MS Royal 14 C. VII, f.8v])

2. Portrait of William II, detail from *The Chronicle of Abingdon*, *c.*1220 (© The British Library Board [Cotton Claudius B. VI, f.124])

3. Bishop Odo with William I and his half-brother Robert of Mortain, detail from the Bayeux Tapestry, before 1082 (Musée de la Tapisserie, Bayeux, France/Bridgeman Images)

4. The Great Seal of William II, illustration from George Lillie Craik, *The Pictorial History of England*, 1846

5. Portrait of Anselm of Canterbury, mid twelfth century (© Bodleian Library, Oxford [MS Auct. D. 2. 6 f.156r])

6. Pope Urban II presiding over the Council of Clermont, illustration from *Le Passage faits outremer*, *c.*1490 (Bibliothèque Nationale, Paris/Bridgeman Images)

7. Silver penny of William II struck at Maldon by Lifsun *c.*1087–90 (© The Trustees of the British Museum)

8. The Holy Face of Lucca, Duomo di San Martino, Lucca (© Stuart Black/Alamy)

9. William II burning a town in Normandy, detail from a French manuscript *c.*1470–80 (Bibliothèque Sainte-Geneviève, Paris [MS 0935, f. 109v]/ Flammarion/Bridgeman Images)

10. Rochester Castle, Kent (© Historic England)

Acknowledgements

In writing this I have been considerably helped by Richard Sharpe's generosity in providing me with both published and unpublished material relating to his forthcoming edition of the writs and charters of William II and Henry I. To Ian Short, the editor and translator of Gaimar's *Estoire des Engleis,* I owe not only his careful reading of my whole text but also his advice and help on translations from French and Latin. All remaining infelicities and inaccuracies are my fault.

Whenever possible I have provided references to modern English translations of quotations from texts written in Old English, French and Latin. These references, however, mean only that the translations given here correspond roughly to those cited.

I would like to thank those who materially helped to see this book through to publication: Anna Hervé, Linden Lawson, Cecilia Mackay and Louise Wilder. Special thanks to Simon Winder who, by allowing me to write about Rufus, gave me the opportunity to re-read the work of a remarkable group of English historians.

Index

Penguin Monarchs

THE HOUSES OF WESSEX AND DENMARK

Athelstan*	Tom Holland
Aethelred the Unready	Richard Abels
Cnut	Ryan Lavelle
Edward the Confessor	David Woodman

THE HOUSES OF NORMANDY, BLOIS AND ANJOU

William I*	Marc Morris
William II*	John Gillingham
Henry I	Edmund King
Stephen*	Carl Watkins
Henry II*	Richard Barber
Richard I*	Thomas Asbridge
John	Nicholas Vincent

THE HOUSE OF PLANTAGENET

Henry III*	Stephen Church
Edward I*	Andy King
Edward II*	Christopher Given-Wilson
Edward III*	Jonathan Sumption
Richard II*	Laura Ashe

THE HOUSES OF LANCASTER AND YORK

Henry IV	Catherine Nall
Henry V*	Anne Curry
Henry VI*	James Ross
Edward IV*	A. J. Pollard
Edward V	Thomas Penn
Richard III	Rosemary Horrox

* Now in paperback

THE HOUSE OF TUDOR

Henry VII	Sean Cunningham
Henry VIII*	John Guy
Edward VI*	Stephen Alford
Mary I*	John Edwards
Elizabeth I*	Helen Castor

THE HOUSE OF STUART

James I*	Thomas Cogswell
Charles I*	Mark Kishlansky
[Cromwell*	David Horspool]
Charles II*	Clare Jackson
James II*	David Womersley
William III & Mary II*	Jonathan Keates
Anne	Richard Hewlings

THE HOUSE OF HANOVER

George I*	Tim Blanning
George II	Norman Davies
George III	Amanda Foreman
George IV	Stella Tillyard
William IV*	Roger Knight
Victoria*	Jane Ridley

THE HOUSES OF SAXE-COBURG & GOTHA AND WINDSOR

Edward VII*	Richard Davenport-Hines
George V*	David Cannadine
Edward VIII*	Piers Brendon
George VI*	Philip Ziegler
Elizabeth II*	Douglas Hurd

* Now in paperback

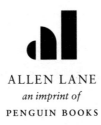

ALLEN LANE
an imprint of
PENGUIN BOOKS

Also Published

David Wallace-Wells, *The Uninhabitable Earth: A Story of the Future*

Randolph M. Nesse, *Good Reasons for Bad Feelings: Insights from the Frontier of Evolutionary Psychiatry*

Anand Giridharadas, *Winners Take All: The Elite Charade of Changing the World*

Richard Bassett, *Last Days in Old Europe: Triste '79, Vienna '85, Prague '89*

Paul Davies, *The Demon in the Machine: How Hidden Webs of Information Are Finally Solving the Mystery of Life*

Toby Green, *A Fistful of Shells: West Africa from the Rise of the Slave Trade to the Age of Revolution*

Paul Dolan, *Happy Ever After: Escaping the Myth of The Perfect Life*

Sunil Amrith, *Unruly Waters: How Mountain Rivers and Monsoons Have Shaped South Asia's History*

Christopher Harding, *Japan Story: In Search of a Nation, 1850 to the Present*

Timothy Day, *I Saw Eternity the Other Night: King's College, Cambridge, and an English Singing Style*

Richard Abels, *Aethelred the Unready: The Failed King*

Eric Kaufmann, *Whiteshift: Populism, Immigration and the Future of White Majorities*

Alan Greenspan and Adrian Wooldridge, *Capitalism in America: A History*

Philip Hensher, *The Penguin Book of the Contemporary British Short Story*

Paul Collier, *The Future of Capitalism: Facing the New Anxieties*

Andrew Roberts, *Churchill: Walking With Destiny*

Tim Flannery, *Europe: A Natural History*

T. M. Devine, *The Scottish Clearances: A History of the Dispossessed, 1600-1900*

Robert Plomin, *Blueprint: How DNA Makes Us Who We Are*

Michael Lewis, *The Fifth Risk: Undoing Democracy*

Diarmaid MacCulloch, *Thomas Cromwell: A Life*

Ramachandra Guha, *Gandhi: 1914-1948*

Slavoj Žižek, *Like a Thief in Broad Daylight: Power in the Era of Post-Humanity*

Neil MacGregor, *Living with the Gods: On Beliefs and Peoples*

Peter Biskind, *The Sky is Falling: How Vampires, Zombies, Androids and Superheroes Made America Great for Extremism*

Robert Skidelsky, *Money and Government: A Challenge to Mainstream Economics*

Helen Parr, *Our Boys: The Story of a Paratrooper*

David Gilmour, *The British in India: Three Centuries of Ambition and Experience*

Jonathan Haidt and Greg Lukianoff, *The Coddling of the American Mind: How Good Intentions and Bad Ideas are Setting up a Generation for Failure*

Ian Kershaw, *Roller-Coaster: Europe, 1950-2017*

Adam Tooze, *Crashed: How a Decade of Financial Crises Changed the World*

Edmund King, *Henry I: The Father of His People*

Lilia M. Schwarcz and Heloisa M. Starling, *Brazil: A Biography*

Jesse Norman, *Adam Smith: What He Thought, and Why it Matters*

Philip Augur, *The Bank that Lived a Little: Barclays in the Age of the Very Free Market*

Christopher Andrew, *The Secret World: A History of Intelligence*

David Edgerton, *The Rise and Fall of the British Nation: A Twentieth-Century History*

Julian Jackson, *A Certain Idea of France: The Life of Charles de Gaulle*

Owen Hatherley, *Trans-Europe Express*

Richard Wilkinson and Kate Pickett, *The Inner Level: How More Equal Societies Reduce Stress, Restore Sanity and Improve Everyone's Wellbeing*

Paul Kildea, *Chopin's Piano: A Journey Through Romanticism*

Seymour M. Hersh, *Reporter: A Memoir*

Michael Pollan, *How to Change Your Mind: The New Science of Psychedelics*

David Christian, *Origin Story: A Big History of Everything*

Judea Pearl and Dana Mackenzie, *The Book of Why: The New Science of Cause and Effect*

David Graeber, *Bullshit Jobs: A Theory*

Serhii Plokhy, *Chernobyl: History of a Tragedy*

Michael McFaul, *From Cold War to Hot Peace: The Inside Story of Russia and America*

Paul Broks, *The Darker the Night, the Brighter the Stars: A Neuropsychologist's Odyssey*

Lawrence Wright, *God Save Texas: A Journey into the Future of America*

John Gray, *Seven Types of Atheism*

Carlo Rovelli, *The Order of Time*

Mariana Mazzucato, *The Value of Everything: Making and Taking in the Global Economy*

Richard Vinen, *The Long '68: Radical Protest and Its Enemies*

Kishore Mahbubani, *Has the West Lost It?: A Provocation*

John Lewis Gaddis, *On Grand Strategy*

Richard Overy, *The Birth of the RAF, 1918: The World's First Air Force*

Francis Pryor, *Paths to the Past: Encounters with Britain's Hidden Landscapes*

Helen Castor, *Elizabeth I: A Study in Insecurity*

Ken Robinson and Lou Aronica, *You, Your Child and School*

Leonard Mlodinow, *Elastic: Flexible Thinking in a Constantly Changing World*

Nick Chater, *The Mind is Flat: The Illusion of Mental Depth and The Improvised Mind*

Michio Kaku, *The Future of Humanity: Terraforming Mars, Interstellar Travel, Immortality, and Our Destiny Beyond*

Thomas Asbridge, *Richard I: The Crusader King*

Richard Sennett, *Building and Dwelling: Ethics for the City*

Nassim Nicholas Taleb, *Skin in the Game: Hidden Asymmetries in Daily Life*

Steven Pinker, *Enlightenment Now: The Case for Reason, Science, Humanism and Progress*

Steve Coll, *Directorate S: The C.I.A. and America's Secret Wars in Afghanistan, 2001 - 2006*

Jordan B. Peterson, *12 Rules for Life: An Antidote to Chaos*

Bruno Maçães, *The Dawn of Eurasia: On the Trail of the New World Order*

Brock Bastian, *The Other Side of Happiness: Embracing a More Fearless Approach to Living*

Ryan Lavelle, *Cnut: The North Sea King*

Tim Blanning, *George I: The Lucky King*

Thomas Cogswell, *James I: The Phoenix King*

Pete Souza, *Obama, An Intimate Portrait: The Historic Presidency in Photographs*

Robert Dallek, *Franklin D. Roosevelt: A Political Life*

Norman Davies, *Beneath Another Sky: A Global Journey into History*

Ian Black, *Enemies and Neighbours: Arabs and Jews in Palestine and Israel, 1917-2017*

Martin Goodman, *A History of Judaism*

Shami Chakrabarti, *Of Women: In the 21st Century*

Stephen Kotkin, *Stalin, Vol. II: Waiting for Hitler, 1928-1941*

Lindsey Fitzharris, *The Butchering Art: Joseph Lister's Quest to Transform the Grisly World of Victorian Medicine*

Serhii Plokhy, *Lost Kingdom: A History of Russian Nationalism from Ivan the Great to Vladimir Putin*

Mark Mazower, *What You Did Not Tell: A Russian Past and the Journey Home*

Lawrence Freedman, *The Future of War: A History*

Niall Ferguson, *The Square and the Tower: Networks, Hierarchies and the Struggle for Global Power*

Matthew Walker, *Why We Sleep: The New Science of Sleep and Dreams*

Edward O. Wilson, *The Origins of Creativity*

John Bradshaw, *The Animals Among Us: The New Science of Anthropology*

David Cannadine, *Victorious Century: The United Kingdom, 1800-1906*

Leonard Susskind and Art Friedman, *Special Relativity and Classical Field Theory*

Maria Alyokhina, *Riot Days*

Oona A. Hathaway and Scott J. Shapiro, *The Internationalists: And Their Plan to Outlaw War*

Chris Renwick, *Bread for All: The Origins of the Welfare State*

Anne Applebaum, *Red Famine: Stalin's War on Ukraine*

Richard McGregor, *Asia's Reckoning: The Struggle for Global Dominance*

Chris Kraus, *After Kathy Acker: A Biography*

Clair Wills, *Lovers and Strangers: An Immigrant History of Post-War Britain*

Odd Arne Westad, *The Cold War: A World History*

Max Tegmark, *Life 3.0: Being Human in the Age of Artificial Intelligence*

Jonathan Losos, *Improbable Destinies: How Predictable is Evolution?*

Chris D. Thomas, *Inheritors of the Earth: How Nature Is Thriving in an Age of Extinction*

Chris Patten, *First Confession: A Sort of Memoir*

James Delbourgo, *Collecting the World: The Life and Curiosity of Hans Sloane*

Naomi Klein, *No Is Not Enough: Defeating the New Shock Politics*

Ulrich Raulff, *Farewell to the Horse: The Final Century of Our Relationship*

Slavoj Žižek, *The Courage of Hopelessness: Chronicles of a Year of Acting Dangerously*

Patricia Lockwood, *Priestdaddy: A Memoir*

Ian Johnson, *The Souls of China: The Return of Religion After Mao*

Stephen Alford, *London's Triumph: Merchant Adventurers and the Tudor City*

Hugo Mercier and Dan Sperber, *The Enigma of Reason: A New Theory of Human Understanding*

Stuart Hall, *Familiar Stranger: A Life Between Two Islands*

Allen Ginsberg, *The Best Minds of My Generation: A Literary History of the Beats*

Sayeeda Warsi, *The Enemy Within: A Tale of Muslim Britain*

Alexander Betts and Paul Collier, *Refuge: Transforming a Broken Refugee System*

Robert Bickers, *Out of China: How the Chinese Ended the Era of Western Domination*

Erica Benner, *Be Like the Fox: Machiavelli's Lifelong Quest for Freedom*

William D. Cohan, *Why Wall Street Matters*

David Horspool, *Oliver Cromwell: The Protector*

Daniel C. Dennett, *From Bacteria to Bach and Back: The Evolution of Minds*